Vanity

THE ART OF
LOOKING GOOD

SIN SERIES

VOLUME VI

Vanity

THE ART OF
LOOKING GOOD

LINDA ABRAMS

RED ROCK PRESS, NEW YORK

Copyright © 2003, by Red Rock Press
ISBN: 0-9669573-4-2
LOC: 2001095472
Published by Red Rock Press
New York, New York
U.S.A.
www.redrockpress.com

Grateful acknowledgement is made for the following:

COVER ART: *Junge Frau Bei Der Toilette* by Giovanni Bellini (1430-1516), Kunsthistorisches Museum, Vienna.

Every reasonable effort has been made to trace and credit the ownership of any copyright- protected material appearing in this book. Any errors or omissions are inadvertent and will be corrected in subsequent editions if the publisher is notified in writing of the mistake.

PRINTED IN HONG KONG

Introduction to Looking Good

Growing up in Pittsburgh, far from any fashion capital, we had a travertine marble shelf where magazines were lined up like dominoes. Next to *Life*, *Time* and *The New Yorker* were a series of fashion magazines—*Vogue*, *Harper's Bazaar* and a funny little newspaper called *Women's Wear Daily*. I loved that rag-trade paper.

My mother, who was a beautiful woman, well and fashionably dressed, told me you should always look good when you go out because "you never know whom you're going to run into." Her admiration for fashion became mine.

So it was not surprising that years later I wound up writing for that little rag-trade paper, then covered Paris and New York fashion shows for the international *Herald Tribune* and was briefly the Fashion Editor for *The Washington Post*.

As a teenager, I embarrassed myself when I wanted to appear to have a perfect body. I'll never forget the time I jumped into a swimming pool while wearing a bathing suit stuffed with rubber falsies. When I rose to the surface so did the falsies, only they were floating on the other side of the pool. And for decades, in the interest of being fashionable, I forced my feet into pointy-toed shoes—and have bunions to prove it.

I have contributed financially multiple times to the welfare of diet centers and health clubs but never actually used my memberships very much. I love clothes and shopping for new ones when the scale obliges. These days, though, I am less interested in extreme "new" looks, and leave the stretch fabrics and spaghetti-strap tops to my daughter. And body piercing is out. I am a fainter who didn't get her ears pierced until she was thirty.

As a fashion journalist, I wanted to know what was new, what was in. And although I would change my skirt length and hairstyle according to the latest look, my definition of "new" either meant a totally original style or a fresh take on revivals from decades past.

It wasn't until I started to put fashion and beauty in perspective and delved back to the long ago and far away that I realized how little is really new, or fully understood how universal the urge to look good is, even if it sometimes requires extreme effort and even pain.

The punk blue hair on a teenager is a revival of a Greek color preference millennia ago; nose jobs were performed back in Renaissance Italy on soldiers who lost them in duels; corsets in the 1800s rearranged women's internal organs; and soot rubbed into knife slashes created art-fully-raised tattoo welts centuries ago, from Japan to Mexico. Pride in one's appearance may define vanity, but it also contributes to our humanity. And so here I celebrate mankind's urge to paint our skin, dye our hair, drape our bodies and decorate ourselves distinctively in the hope that someone else will acknowledge the effort with a raise, a date, a higher position in the tribe, or simply a nod to the art of looking good.

—LINDA ABRAMS

In memory of my mother
Eadie

TABLE OF CONTENTS

CHAPTER ONE

REFLECTIONS

OVER TIME

As children we all loved to hate Snow White's wicked stepmother, a vain and beautiful queen who was so proud she could not bear the thought that anyone in the world had greater beauty. Her famous question: "Mirror, mirror on the wall/Who is the fairest of us all?" demanded only one answer. No chance to ask the audience or call a friend on that one. Snow White was doomed when the mirror gave the queen the bad news. We can imagine the aging, raging queen yelling back: "Is that your final answer?"

The good news is that the world is—and long has been—full of second chances, enabling us to believe that any mirror would dub us *fair* if we could iron out the wrinkles and find the right hairdresser.

Vanity emerged early in one real live queen, Marie of Romania, who thought she was ravishingly beautiful. In her autobiography she declared herself hot stuff even as a child: "At the age of six, while playing in my mother's room, I looked in the mirror for the first time, and I realized, in me, beauty had found a true friend." No self-doubt there.

That potent magnifier of self-revelation, the looking glass, reflects consciousness of ourselves from a young age. Some babies have mirrors hanging above their cribs to get a head start on separating themselves from their mothers—early self-awareness. No matter how fleeting the gaze, a look in the mirror reveals who we are—gender, race, age, beauty or lack of it. When the looks of Elizabeth I started to go, she sat in the dark and banished mirrors from her palace.

© PHOTO DISC, INC.

10

The Myth and The Mirror

Man's preoccupation with his own image has created myths—the most famous being that of Narcissus, the handsome and vain young man in Greek mythology whose story left us with a name labeling vanity and self-love.

One day, while hunting in the mountains, *Narcissus* came to a clear pool of water and leaned over to drink from it. Seeing his own reflection, he fell in love with himself. Not a great idea. When he bent to kiss his own reflection, the image disappeared. He died of grief by the pool, weeping for his lost image. Perhaps, if he had had a hand mirror around, he could have left his poolside post.

Watery Reflection: Narcissus looked too closely at himself and disappeared.

DETAIL FROM *ECHO AND NARCISSUS* BY JOHN WILLIAM WATERHOUSE.

FIRST GLANCES

Benaki Museum, Athens, Greece

As household items, mirrors go back to the Iron Ages. The Celtic people favored the mirror as a useful accessory. Mirrors have been found in well-preserved Celtic graves along with manicure tools and shaving equipment. The hairy ape-man grunge look was out. Neatness counted. The mirror certainly would have helped a Celtic woman arrange her sophisticated hairdo—braids adorned with ornaments.

The Greeks attributed the invention of the mirror to the god of fire and metal, Hephaestus. In *The Odyssey*, Odysseus, disguised as a peddler, carries bronze mirrors in his bag of trinkets to the court of King Lycomedes.

In the 5th century B.C., Corinthians gazed at themselves in small polished discs of copper and tin attached to handles, the backs decorated with mythical scenes. The oldest mirrors, dating back more than 6000 years, were discovered in Catal Huyuk, Turkey. They are disks made of obsidian, a highly-reflective volcanic rock. Heavy but helpful. The Egyptians made metal (mostly copper) mirrors five thousand years ago.

The reverse side of s Greek bronze mirror, circa 330 B.C., reveals what a treasure it was.

Mirrors have played roles in both theology and the black arts, as reflectors of the past and predictors of the future. In 296 A.D., the Wei emperor King Ai was buried with several hundred bronze mirrors, all facing up, to ward off any evil spirits looking down on him.

Native Americans had low-tech mirrors when Europeans first encountered them. Women of the isolated Tsimshian in British Columbia, for example, wore slate disk pendants around their necks. When a woman felt the urge to look at herself, she simply licked the slate to dampen it and held it up to the sun to check out her face.

Blue Ribbon Braggart #1

"To love oneself is the beginning of a lifelong romance."
—Oscar Wilde.

Hall of Mirrors

Polished metal mirrors remained common in Europe during the Middle Ages. The mirror as we know it—the queen's "looking glass," silvered with lead or tin-foil to reflect perfectly—was invented in the 13th century in Venice and quickly became an expensive, glamorous decoration.

Monkey See, Monkey Like

Is striving to look good a primal urge? In the late 1960s, George Gallop put chimps to the mirror-image test. He painted odorless red lines above the eyebrows of sleeping monkeys and made mirrors available to them when they awoke. The chimpanzees noticed the cosmetic changes to their foreheads and were curious about them; they touched the red lines and smelled their hands and even examined their teeth. The chimps also made fashion statements by draping vines around their necks and placing vegetables on their heads. Cha. Cha. Cha. Gallop concluded that chimps, like their primate cousins, us, are "self-aware" in the personal appearance department. A smart chimp knows enough to question a cosmetic smear on the forehead and put a leafy boa around the neck, instead. It simply looks better.

The Venetians produced fine-quality mirrors; eventually London and Paris followed. The princely Hall of Mirrors (built from 1678-1684) at the royal palace of Versailles was considered an outstanding technical achievement. Seventeen huge casement windows faced a wall of seventeen mirrors (made of 306 panes that blended together and appeared to be a single pane). The effect expanded the room so that it seemed almost infinite. The enormous mirrored panels were tremendously expensive and difficult to install—but worth it. Louis XIV (The Sun King) could stroll down his gallery leading his court as the mirrors reflected the showy red feathers in his tricorne (he was the only man in the realm permitted to wear his hat indoors), his gold-encrusted costume and the jewels of his guests in all their splendor.

Two hundred years later, Versailles was outshone by the Bavarian castle built by Ludwig II: "Hi, I'm King Ludwig and you're not." He didn't say that, but he could have. What Ludwig actually proclaimed was, "I am the taste."

Self-Reflections

"I had a nasty piece of land that brought in nothing but wheat; I sold it, in return I got a mirror." —COUNTESS DE FIESQUE, 1699

"I was France." —CHARLES DE GAULLE

"I am the greatest." —MUHAMMED ALI

"When I was a child, my mother said to me, 'If you become a soldier, you'll be a general. If you become a monk, you'll end up as the Pope.' Instead, I became a painter and wound up as Picasso." —PABLO PICASSO

"I may have faults, but being wrong ain't one of them." —JAMES HOFFA

REFLECTIVE ACQUISITIONS

The Hall of Mirrors also initiated a bourgeois taste for a new fixture in the home. Manuals of social etiquette declared the mirror an indispensable piece of furniture, whether as part of an armoire or in a small compact in a young woman's trousseau. Comtesse de Gence took

A heavenly image in the glass appears;
To that she bends, to that her eyes she rears.
Th' inferior priestess, at her altar's side,
Trembling begins the sacred rites of Pride . . .
Puffs, powders, patches, Bibles, billet-doux.
Now awful beauty puts on all its arms;
The Fair each moment rises in her charms,
Repairs her smiles, awakens ev'ry grace,
And calls forth all the wonders of her face . . .
—from *Rape of the Lock*, 1712, by *ALEXANDER POPE*

THE RAPE BY AUBREY BEARDSLEY, ILLUSTRATION FROM *THE RAPE OF THE LOCK*

the mirror into the 19th century bathroom. "There are never too many mirrors in a bathroom. One has to be able to see herself from head to toe in every direction," she wrote in *Le Cabinette de Toilette*.

But from nearly the beginning, glass mirrors had their critics. In the early 17th century, men and women of fashion liked to wear small mirrors attached to the belt by little silver chains. God-fearing church leaders found this particularly objectionable: "Those who minister to vainglory and to appearance with the aid of a mirror fuel a malady of the soul," wrote cleric L. Beyerlinck in 1631.

In the 17th and 18th centuries, the Japanese wore mirrors pinned to their sleeves, which conveniently allowed them to check their faces as they strolled down the street.

The Art of Staring Back

The vain and sensuous girl in Hans Memling's (c. 1430-1494) painting, *Vanity*, holds a round convex mirror in her hand while she stands in all her sinful nudity in an open field of flowers. How rude! Italian painter Pier Francesco Bissolo (1492-1554) depicted Vanity staring at herself while combing her long hair before a mirror.

Four centuries later, the dreamy look of Norman Rockwell's *Girl at the Mirror* captures a moment of passage: A girl, doll thrown on the floor and fashion magazine on her lap, seems

Girl in the Mirror by Norman Rockwell.

to be assessing her future as a woman. She could be right out of the French comedy *La Dispute* (1744) by Pierre de Marivaux, whose teenage heroine, Eglee, sees herself for the first time in a mirror and says, "I could spend my life contemplating myself."

A mirror image also claims the time of male characters like Dan Gregory, the self-absorbed artist in Kurt Vonnegut's 1987 novel, *Bluebeard*, who has 52 mirrors in his studio.

The black and white photos of photographer Bruce Davidson reveal 1950s teenage boys primping their greasy pompadours in the reflection of a plate glass window.

We all use the mirror as a personal spy and summon it to judge us, young or old, male or female. Am I still the fairest of them all?

"Vanity of vanities, saith the Preacher, vanity of vanities: all *is* vanity"
—ECCLESIASTES 1:2

Twentieth Century Fox, 1989

Final Take

"You look fine!"
     –Alicia (JERRY HALL)

"I didn't ask!"
     –The Joker (JACK NICHOLSON),
Batman (Twentieth Century Fox), 1989

CHAPTER TWO

THE SKIN

As Canvas

Our skin is our first blank canvas, ready for any artistic enhancement. Body art is a visual language that not only tells us something about a culture's sense of beauty, it also identifies an individual's place in society. Pacific Islanders traditionally tattooed their bodies to declare their rank, while Indian women dye their skin for the marriage ceremony. War paint may scare away the enemy and eye glitter may attract a suitor. Body art allows for individual creativity or a chance for reinvention or rebellion.

We paint our faces, torsos and limbs with as much artistic skill as we can muster—whether from crushed sesame seeds, a tube of designer lipstick, or a tattoo needle. Our desire to outline and draw and color apparently has been in our nature since the beginning of recorded time; the impulse to create art on our bodies helps define our humanity.

Archeologists have found ornaments and makeup palettes, even ceramics depicting painted bodies, in caves and at burial sites around the world. The word "cosmetics" comes from the Greek word "*cosmos*," meaning adornment.

This gorgeously tatooed Pacific islander was drawn by an early 19th-century European voyager. The flesh of this gentleman is as decorated as his outrigger paddle.

"NOUKAHIWA" FROM *MOEURS, USAGES ET COSTUMES DE TOUS LES PEUPLES DU MONDE* BY AUGUSTE WAHLEN, BRUSSELS, 1845.

Some European explorers and traders who discovered painted faces and boldly marked bodies in the Americas, Africa and the Pacific thought them the marks of "savages." These scornful men understood neither their own cultural histories nor the meanings underlying the extravagant designs they beheld. As always, it all depends on who's looking.

In Brazil, Eyiguayegui Indians told missionaries they were stupid for not wearing paint—without paint, a man was no better than a beast. The nomadic Wodaabe people of the Niger region take great pride in their good looks. But it's the men who compete every year in a beauty contest to win the affection of a prospective wife. In preparation, the men spend hours applying red ochre to their faces and black kohl around their eyes and on their lips, and use white lines to elongate their noses. Their hair is dressed with cowrie shells and ostrich feathers. They preen and dance in front of their female judges, hoping to get a nudge or wink from one of them—signifying success.

In Ethiopia, a Karo woman demonstrates her artistic prowess by creating a facial mask of exquisite detail. She paints her entire face with white chalk, powdered yellow rock and iron ore to imitate the spotted feathers of a guinea fowl.

Australian Aborigines use natural earth pigments to color their bodies and announce their close relationship with the environment. For funerals, the Tiwi (on Bathurst and Melville islands) decorate their whole bodies and faces with patterns in complex designs to mask their identity so the deceased cannot reclaim them.

War paint has been known on every inhabited continent. When Julius Caesar and his Roman legions crossed the English Channel in 55 B.C. to get a good look at the Celts, they were awed by their foes' cosmetic fierceness. "All Britons dye themselves with woad, which makes them blue so that in battle their appearance is more terrible," Caesar wrote.

The Celtic cosmetic was indigo derived from plants similar to those that grew on the

Food For Thought

Do I serve it or wear it? For centuries we have employed fruits and vegetables to keep our bodies beautiful. Olive oil is one of the world's oldest skin softeners; mashed avocado is a deliriously expensive alternative. Elizabethan women depended on a facial mask of asparagus roots and goat's milk, rubbed on the face with warm bread.

Mashed papaya is said to remove dead skin; a mask of boiled carrots and honey on the face allegedly diminishes blemishes. Recommended (but not by me!) are salt scrubs to make your skin glow. Placing iced cucumber slices on the eyes (watch out for seeds), reportedly takes away puffiness after you've had a good cry. The chocolate mud bath (not advised for claustrophobics) once enjoyed a vogue as a head-to-toe skin moisturizer.

European continent and Asia.

War paint once worn by the Catawba of South Carolina intimidated their enemies. One white circle around one eye and a black pattern around the other highlighted their black-painted faces. The Cherokee found them fearsome.

Today, soldiers paint their faces to hide and blend in with their surroundings. During both world wars, hundreds of artists served as camouflage experts who advised guys how to apply their green and black makeup in irregular patterns. While the purpose isn't party chic, a muddy-faced male in a movie or a fashion layout has become a symbol of a real man with virility. And a female fashion model with a dirty face signifies a tough girl attracted to danger, even if she's wearing a $3000 artfully ripped dress instead of an infantry uniform. It may take hours to get ready for the party or a planned attack, but when you walk in, the first impression takes only a minute.

HONOR OF HENNA

"Oh, friends, come and decorate my hands with *mehndi* [henna], write my beloved's name . . ." sing bridesmaids in India.

This natural maroon adornment, which often marks special occasions, honors a woman's rites of passage. The glorious cosmetic of the Near East is made from the crushed leaves of the henna plant, mixed with ingredients such as tea, lemon juice and eucalyptus oil into a fragrant paste. For centuries, it has been applied with artistry to a woman's hands and feet. Since its designs wash away with water and time, it's a temporary tattoo.

Elaborate designs vary according to locale and religious custom. Peacocks and lacy paisleys, flowers and geometrics inspired by local architecture, help transport a woman from one stage of life to another. In southern India, a circular pattern decorates the center of the palm. The Sudanese of Africa employ henna to create delicate butterflies and fish.

Henna decoration is often a woman's prenuptial party activity; sometimes the prospective mother-in-law applies the first dot, a symbol permitting the bride to make herself beautiful for her groom.

Ancient Egyptians used henna to color the nails and hair of

BIG EYES/BIG LAUGHS

Number 8 on David Letterman's 1988 list, Top Ten Mr. Wizard Experiments: "Taking a core sample of Tammy Faye Bakker's mascara."

corpses on their way to becoming mummies. The Woodstock generation of the 1960s adopted henna as part of their "natural" look. Henna is found in many contemporary hair dyes and conditioners.

Enduring Engraving

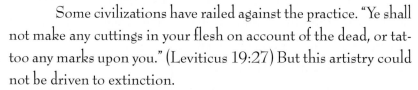

The real tattoo, the one that hurts to put on and doesn't come off, at one time or another has been applied by placing pigment under the skin with thorns, bones, small rakes, knives, steel needles and brass pens. Tattoos are found on 2000-year-old Egyptian mummies. Ancient Romans tattooed slaves and criminals.

Some civilizations have railed against the practice. "Ye shall not make any cuttings in your flesh on account of the dead, or tattoo any marks upon you." (Leviticus 19:27) But this artistry could not be driven to extinction.

In 1595, when the Spanish explorer Alvaro de Mendaña blundered onto the Marquesas Islands (now part of Tahiti), he discovered ornately tattooed natives. Mendaña's only reaction was to kill several hundred of them. In 1769, when Captain James Cook landed on the same island, he and the scientific Joseph Banks actually bothered to find out why the natives wore tattoos.

A Maori tattoo from Capt. Cook's own journal

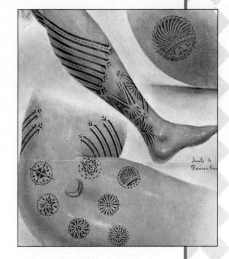

Various tattoo designs noted by botanist Joseph Banks, who accompanied Captain Cook on his 18th-century Pacific voyages

The geometric tattoo designs displayed by the Polynesians signified their place in society; the more powerful the man, the more elaborate the markings that were tapped into his skin with a miniature rake. Highly ornamental tattooing was commonplace in the South Pacific. The Maori of New Zealand marked their faces with shallow colored grooves in complex curved and swirling designs to indicate tribal status.

Tattooing seems to have been meaningfully in vogue almost everywhere except China. Some Native American men were tattooed to celebrate their strength and bravery. Soot has been rubbed into knife slashes in the skin of various peoples of Mexico, Nigeria, Japan and Tunisia—often in the service of beauty. The Berber women of Morocco decorate their chins, foreheads and cheeks with blue tattoos to ward off evil spirits.

Stimulated by Polynesian and, eventually, Japanese tattoo artists, sailors brought tattooing to European and American port cities. In the West, displaying a tattoo was the mark of street gangs, the rough adventurer, or the otherwise rebellious. In Japan, elaborate dragons, demons and legendary warriors were considered protection from evil and death. In the late 1800s, a "progressive" Japanese government banned tattooing, arresting artists and confiscating their tools. But an underground life of tattoo artists (some were fine painters and printmakers) nonetheless thrived.

Tattoos extended to the English upper classes in the late 19th century. There are reports of men gathering after dinner in their country homes and taking off their shirts to show off their trophy tattoos. This display was not confined to men. Winston Churchill's mother, Lady Randolph Churchill (the American beauty, Jenny Jerome), had a snake tattooed around her wrist as a permanent bracelet.

In 1948, a high-ranking officer in General MacArthur's Occupation government saw an exquisite tattoo by a famous Japanese artist and demanded to meet him. When the officer was informed that tattooing was banned, he ordered the law revoked and restored tattooing to its rank among other Japanese arts.

As an American 20th-century tattoo artist, Brooklyn Blackie, put it, "A tattoo is wearing the soul on the outside."

Kintaro and Maple Leaves: This contemporary tattoo stars the folkloric Japanese boy god, Kintaro, wrestling with a giant carp.

PHOTO BY SANDI FELLMAN, 1984

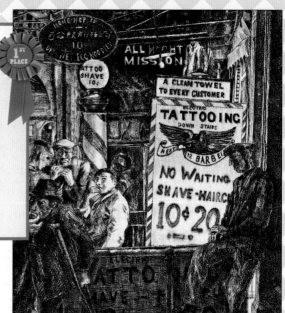

By Reginald March

Blue Ribbon Braggart # 2

"The Electric Rembrandt"
—Coney Island tattoo artist Brooklyn Blackie's self-description, circa 1948

In the Jaws of Beauty

At a small country train station in New York State one day last year, two middle-aged single women were talking about how hard it was to meet a man these days. "All I want," said one woman, "is a man with all his teeth."

Judging a potential date or mate by a smile is a long-standing practice. Since antiquity, believe it or not, replacements have been around to help people flash the best smile. However, the standards of what constituted best have varied. Twenty-seven hundred years ago, rich Etruscans indulged in false teeth made of ivory or bone, skillfully secured with gold bridgework. Elsewhere, the rich sometimes preferred to flaunt their wealth with teeth of gold, silver, agate or mother of pearl. Where human teeth set the beauty standard, the poor sometimes sold off their pearly whites to the rich.

In southwestern Mississippi, Natchez women made their teeth alluring by rubbing them daily with wood ash and tobacco. In the mid-1700s, a French missionary named Gravier found that "Most [Natchez] have black teeth, which are considered beautiful." Pre-Columbian Mexicans liked to decorate their teeth by inlaying semiprecious stones, such as turquoise, or bits of pyrite. Teeth have been filed, grooved, and removed to conform with cultural standards of fine fangs. Malavedans from Southern India filed their teeth into points; the Ivory Coast Baules artistically removed half of each front incisor so that when they smiled, they revealed a black triangle.

Although current American cosmetic dentistry includes pricey bleach rituals, unadorned white does not appeal to everyone, particularly a substrata of trendy black youth, who embrace the look of teeth as jewels. Web sites sell tooth caps of silver, platinum and gold studded with crushed diamonds, rubies or blue zircons, which can be set into glittering initials or arranged as the American flag.

A few years ago, author Nuala O'Faolain claimed little dental self-improvement existed in Ireland: "You're supposed to assert your gritty authenticity by a display of yellowing, crooked, brownish bits and pieces of teeth that have the amazing merit of being untouched by the twentieth century."

PAINTED LADIES (AND GENTS)

Although in the Bible, Elijah the Tishbite warned that painted ladies would end up like Jezebel, "as dung upon the face of the field"(Kings 9:37) and the women of Jerusalem

were told: "though thou rentest thy face with painting, in vain shalt thou make thyself fair" (Jeremiah 4:31), facial cosmetics did not disappear from the Judeo-Christian-Islamic tradition.

Long ago, Bedouin women made rouge and lip color from the fine red powder of safflower blossoms. Today, lipstick may brighten a mouth under a veil.

The all-time cosmetics queen, though, didn't have to deal with strictures against enhancing her looks. Cleopatra, Queen of the Nile, sailed the Cydnus River to meet Mark Anthony, dripping in a peacock palette of makeup and perfume. (And who can doubt she did a massive touch-up before Anthony appeared?) Cleopatra's rouge was yellow ochre, made from a fine clay containing iron ore, and her lips were tinted with carmine, a purplish-red pigment made from the dried bodies of female beetles. To add a little more glamour, like other highborn Egyptian women, her face was probably glittered with an ointment made from crushed iridescent beetle shells or mother of pearl and mixed with paint. Under the dazzle, Cleo was the first to use ceruse—white-lead paint mixed with vinegar to form a paste—to cover her face, breasts and neck.

Millennia later, Elizabeth I made the white face fashionable again. The downside to the chalky complexion was that the potion contained heavy metals that were absorbed through the skin. The ironic result: premature wrinkles or worse—death.

But the Elizabethans couldn't have known that, could they?

In 168 A.D., Galen (Greek-born physician to the gladiators) wrote: "Women who often paint themselves with mercury or lead, though they be very young, they presently turn old and withered and have wrinkled faces like an ape."

Incidentally, face paint was an equal-opportunity toxin. Nero whitened his face with ceruse before blackening his eyelashes with kohl and reddening his lips and cheeks from the moss of rock lichen.

Some high-styled Roman men copied Nero, just as 16th-century ladies followed the latest cosmetic style of their queen. These English beauties had no use for freckles, either. They mixed elder leaves, birch sap and sulfur and applied the ointment to their faces by candlelight. In the morning they removed the mixture with fresh butter.

Pallor was prized in much of Europe among those who wished to distinguish themselves from suntanned laborers. Bohemian ladies not only covered their faces in poison, they migrated like birds to drink from arsenic springs, which further paled their complexions. (Arsenic was also favored by fragile Victorian women, who needed to ingest greater and greater amounts to achieve the desired "look"; there is some anecdotal evidence to suggest that a deep kiss from one of these pallid beauties could prove near-fatal to their lovers.)

Was this fair to their menfolk? In 1711, the *London Spectator* published the pleas of a man who wanted a separation from his wife on grounds of deception: "... enamored as I was of her fair forehead, neck and arms, as well as the bright jet of her hair: but to my astonishment, I find they were all the effect of art. When she wakes in the morning, she scarce seems young enough to be the mother of her whom I carried to bed the night before."

That same year, Parliament passed legislation voiding marriages of men who were lured into unions by cosmetics.

Heavy cosmetics even went out of style during much of the 19th century while women recovered from the harsh chemical blush of beauty; when they reappeared they were marketed with health in mind. In the 1890s, Helena Rubenstein, a Polish immigrant to the United States, sold her jars of hope (12 pots of her mother's skin cleanser) as "health aids."

MUSTACHE AND THE MAIDEN

Most women in the world try to kill a hair the moment it appears on the upper lip. But in the late 1800s in the far northern provinces of Japan, Ainu girls started on tattooed mustaches at the age of two or three. Every year a few incisions were made around the child's mouth and soot was rubbed into the cuts. Her mustache was expanded until she married.

THE EYES HAVE IT

In addition to her other artificial charms, Cleopatra's high-drama makeup included double eye shadows—blue galena on the top lid, green malachite on the bottom—and eyes and brows lined with kohl, a jet black (antimony) powder mixed with animal fat to outline the eyes with a dark lustrous look.

Kohl impressively makes the whites of the eyes stand out, and was also used by men. However, kohl, still the eyeliner of choice in many places, may have plusses beyond beauty. It protects eyes against the glare of a merciless sun, wards off flies and is considered a disinfectant against eye dis-

Soap, which cognoscenti say, dries out facial tissue, is widely used to create the fresh canvas.

ease. What's more, it's thought to be a spiritual guard against "the evil eye" (a belief that suffering or infection can be caused by a pointedly aimed hateful or lustful glance).

The Egyptians were so enamored of their cosmetics that they took them with them to the grave. King Tut's tomb, like those of his kin, was filled with makeup to please the gods. Underneath their wraps, mummies are elaborately made up. Back in the day of the pharaohs, rich and poor used makeup; what separated them was the quality of containers they were stored in: humbler graves contained galena in conch shells, hollow reeds, or simple leather or canvas bags; the rich stored their makeup in ivory or jewel-decorated jars.

Several historic eye enhancers could have gone in for some serious lab tests. Shadows often contained lead or antimony sulfide. A fatal stare from an English lady might be literal. Fashionable eyes sparkled with enlarged pupils achieved by drops of belladonna juice from the deadly nightshade plant.

And, for that matter, a kiss on a blushing cheek could be dangerous. Red dyes for cheeks and lips carried mercuric sulfide.

Flutter Flattery

Eyelash-dying was popular in much of the Roman Empire, approved of by no less an authority than Ovid, author of *The Art of Beauty*, who reminded his compatriots: "With sufficient neglect, Venus would look like a hag . . . There's nothing amiss about darkening the eyes with mascara."

CONTINENTAL REMEDY

Flamboyant Irish-born beauty and "Spanish dancer," Lola Montez, fled Europe for the United States when she was little over 30. A decade later she compiled her cosmetics advice in a handy tome for aspiring American beauties. It included a topical lotion for stimulating bosom growth and this recommendation for flexibility in ladies who exercised:

8 ounces fat of stag or deer

6 ounces Florence oil

3 ounces virgin wax

1 ounce musk

$1/2$ pint white brandy

4 ounces rosewater

"Put the fat, oil and wax into a well-glazed earthen vessel, and let them simmer over a slow fire until they are assimilated; then pour in the other ingredients, and let the whole gradually cool, when it will be fit for use. This mixture, frequently and thoroughly rubbed upon the body on going to bed, will impart a remarkable degree of elasticity to the muscles. In the morning, after this preparation has been used, the body should be thoroughly wiped with a sponge, dampened with cold water."

False eyelashes were promoted by none other than movie director D.W. Griffith. While filming *Intolerance* in 1916, he wanted actress Seena Owen to have longer lashes, so he had a wigmaker fashion some to glue onto Owen's eyelids. The movie was a flop and false eyelashes didn't really take off (or begin to fall off in increasing numbers) until 1966. That's when English model Twiggy looked back at us so naturally from the pages of fashion magazines with dark eye fringe as long as her miniskirt.

Today, eyelashes also come in assorted colors studded with rhinestones. But fakes should be eschewed on somber occasions. When newspaper columnist Cindy Adams attended the funeral of her husband, comedian Joey Adams, she reportedly explained, "I can't cry. I'm wearing false eyelashes."

Nailing It Down

The human nail has been fashionably colored, clipped, filed, elongated, polished and buffed to the mirrored shine of a new car since the Chinese invented nail lacquer five millennia ago. Various polishes evolved from acacia tree gum, beeswax, egg whites and gelatin.

During the Chou Dynasty (circa 600 B.C.), nail color announced social class.

Royals wore only gold and silver and, later, black or red lacquer, while commoners were only permitted pale tones.

The Chinese attached superstition to nail clipping. Cutting nails at night invited unwelcome visits from the dead. Nail grooming was strictly a daytime activity; clippings were carefully collected and disposed of in secret places to prevent curses from ancient ghosts.

Fingernail length also established rank. Mandarin men cultivated extremely long, curled nails, demonstrating their exemption from manual labor. Manchu women protected their status symbols by wearing fingernail covers that were delicately carved and inlaid with gold, gems and silver.

In the thousands of years before Chinese polish went international, fashionables elsewhere contented themselves with meek nail stains. So it was that ancient Greek and Egyptian beauties sported rust-colored, henna-coated fingertips. Their European and American successors eventually adopted a variety of scented, red fingernail dyes. Not until 1925 was the first real nail polish, in a rosy red color, sold in the United States. Moralists met the innovation with a warning to women not to paint their nails in "garish color."

Acrylic nail extensions and fiberglass wraps are less than three decades old. The popularity of jellybean colors, such as green, blue or yellow, is much more recent. By the 1990s, nail tech had advanced to the point that nail professionals needed their own space. Over 25,000 nail salons opened in the United States in 1993 alone. Nail art, with refinements such as intricate mini-designs, is the explosive cosmetic art form of our day.

As Marks & Spencer heiress Rebecca Sieff told *Vanity Fair* in 2002, "I don't paint my nails everyday, but I never don't have painted nails. Ever, ever, ever."

Whole Body Works

Indigenous North Americans smeared their skin with softening animal fats to repel mosquitoes and gnats. Egyptians found natural sunscreen oils. To keep their skin smooth, Egyptian women bathed in milk and honey, but only Cleopatra is said to have indulged in a bath of red wine. Nero's wife, Poppaea Sabina, traveled with 400 she-asses to assure a supply of milk for her facials and baths.

Romans of all classes adapted spa treatments devised by the Assyrians and Egyptians. They dipped into a heated pool the size of a football field and jumped in and out of fragrant steam rooms to cleanse themselves, but it was the Turks, who would give their name to steam cleaning. A traditional first step of the Turkish bath was skin buffing with sand. In the hot steam chambers, abrasive olive-oil soaps were used to exfoliate and massage bodies. In the women's baths, masks of muddy henna were also used as moisturizing facials.

Almost all of today's pricey spa treatments are said to derive from some ancient beauty miracle. An exception might be butt sandblasting, where the skin, from mid-cheek to the knees, is pelted with little aluminum crystals and then sucked off with a tiny vacuum cleaner. Great idea if you're planning to expose your behind in a string bikini, although it apparently feels like being scraped with a nail file. Bottoms up!

FINAL TAKE

"A spa? Isn't that kind of like your mother ship?"
—Attorney to law student Elle Woods (REESE WITHERSPOON), *Legally Blonde* (MGM), 2001

CHAPTER THREE

HEADY

CONCEPTS

air, the crowning ornament, has been exalted for its length and gloss in fact and in fairy tale—Rapunzel, Rapunzel, let down your long hair! Any student of medieval towers will tell you she had to have at least a good seventy-five feet of it.

Even St. Paul approved of long hair: "If a woman has long hair, it is her glory." (I Corinthians 11:15)

Baudelaire swoons in his poem, *Her Hair*: "Strong tresses be the swell that carries me/I dream upon your sea of amber/Of dazzling sails, of oarsmen, masts and flames."

Shakespeare's sonnet, *The Rape of Lucrece*, sings: "Her hair like golden thread played with her breath."

Other animals may pick nits from their hair, but we are the only species who cuts it, dyes it, braids it, dusts it and wears fake copies of it. If tresses are a woman's glory, a thick head of hair is a man's sign of virility and dignity. Samson's long hair signified his prowess, until Delilah surreptitiously sheared it off.

What's underneath the turban of a Sikh is a long, coiled braid. The hair under a Moslem's turban or headdress may be somewhat shorter (and messier), but his long beard may be considered to mark his piety. After liberation from Taliban rule, many Afghani men flocked to the barber.

Long before blonde meant bombshell, Europeans considered light hair both desirable and innocent. The Virgin was often painted as a blonde, although it's far more likely a Semitic woman had dark hair.

DETAIL FROM *MADONNA COL BAMBINO E DUE ANGELI* BY FILIPPO LIPPI (1406-1469).

This proud Native American hairstyle outdoes any punk Mohawk look.

Long shiny hair defines youth and good health, which is a part of desirability, i.e., beauty. Centuries before chemotherapy left some cancer treatment victims temporarily bald, people noticed that the ravages of nutritional deficiencies and diseases stole their hair. Genetic legacy in advancing age, of course, may do the same.

People in almost every society have the need to do something with their hair, if only to keep it out of their eyes. Pre-Columbian societies were creative with hair. Aztec women of Mexico braided their long dark tresses with colored pieces of cotton thread and wound them round their heads. Incas had evenly cut hair wrapped five times with a wide headband of woven wool. The Mohawks shaved their hair into the cockscomb. In Virginia, Powhatan Indians shaved the right side of their heads and let the hair on the left side grow long.

The men of Suebi, an ancient Germanic tribe, made themselves look taller by tying their hair in a knot on the crown of their heads, thereby terrifying their enemies in battle.

In the first century B.C., high-class Gauls (both men and women) dyed their long hair red to indicate their rank, according to contemporaneous Greek historian Diodorus Siculus. The conquering Romans made them cut their hair as a sign of submission.

Hair may announce a passage in life or symbolize humility. Boys in ancient Greece cut

Ladies in Blue, Heraklion Museum, Greece

How long have women been fussing with their hair? This ancient fresco from the Knossos Palace on Crete shows beautifully coifed ladies.

their hair short when they reached adolescence. Male Brahmin children between the ages of one and three have their hair shaved by priests to ward off evil, leaving the boy with only a small tuft on his crown.

Hindu adults shave their heads in order to participate in the *Kumbha Mela*, a spiritual pilgrimage to the banks of the Ganges River at Allahabad.

Celtic and Roman clergymen wore only a ring of hair encircling shaved scalps; the tonsure lived on in Christian monks. The shaved scalps of Buddhist monks also symbolize their renouncing of worldly goods and rejection of personal vanity.

Fundamentalist Moslem men believe that Allah will pull them up to heaven by their single long lock of hair that sprouts from a bald head.

At various times, matrons in medieval Europe wore caps, pointed hats or hair veils, but eligible girls exposed long flowing tresses to attract a man. Today, an orthodox, married Jewish woman saves the luxury of her locks for her husband; in public her hair is covered either by a wig or scarf. In much of the Islamic world, a veil or scarf is required of a modest woman, married or single.

Waxing and Whining

According to the Koran, a hirsute male offends. By shaving his body hair, a man demonstrates by his clean appearance his readiness to meet Allah.

Ancient Romans didn't like body hair, either. Seneca, whose lodgings were over the Roman steam baths installed in Britain, reported, "You have to imagine the depilator giving his falsetto shriek to advertise his presence and never silent except when making somebody else scream by plucking hair from his armpits."

In the brave new world of male vanity, Actor Robin Williams is obviously not ashamed of his body hair, but some men hate the furry feeling and go for chest and back waxing: Rip it out with hot wax on a gauze pad; rub skin down with oil.

Many American women consider it unattractive to have hair on their legs, underarms and bikini lines. Shaving lasts a day or two: waxing, six weeks. More durable results are often desired, especially for facial hair. The FDA considers only electrolysis a permanent hair remover. A needle is put into the hair root and surrounding cells and delivers a low-level buzz of electricity directly to the follicle, destroying it. The hair will *not* grow back, but one has to endure the time-consuming bore of doing one hair at a time.

Enter laser treatments: A light beam is focused down toward the hair roots and follicles and transformed into heat energy. Each pulse demolishes about ten hairs. It is a possible treatment for any body hair except the eyebrows—too close to the eyes. Although laser treatments are very fast, multiple zap sessions may be necessary and after some months, new hair may sprout. Since the laser beam's target is hair melanin (which gives darkness), light hair tends to stay rooted.

The indignity of most hair-removal techniques usually includes nothing more dire than flashes of pain and fleeting skin redness (although there can be other unanticipated negative consequences when needle wielders are clumsy). But, oh, the dignity of feeling silky smooth.

Politics of Hair

The pigtail or queue was the preferred hairstyle of the Manchu who became China's rulers in the 17th century. The long braid resembled a horsetail and thus symbolized the speed and endurance of the animal that had made the Manchu conquest possible. In 1645, the Manchu regent Dorgon ordered all men to shave their fore scalps and grow a queue, on *pain of death*. That worked. In 1911, when revolutionaries toppled the Manchu Empire, Chinese men cut off their queues.

A 16th-century French king started his own trickle-down hair trend. Short hair, beards and mustaches became the rage for men after Francis I accidentally torched his long locks. Francis's facial hair may have concealed scars; soon, every stylish Frenchman had a beard, too.

In recent decades, male politicians have had to think as much about their hair as Francis I and his followers did. Lay the blame on John F. Kennedy, who startled trend watchers by campaigning without a hat, robustly reviving the link between prowess and a healthy mop. Hats don't cut it unless the politician is on a construction site or at a baseball game. Otherwise, it's a suspicious cover up; the public wants to know not just what's in a candidate's head, but what's on it, too.

Hairy Times/20th Century

1905—Charles Nessler, a German, invents permanent wave. It takes 12 hours to go curly.

1909—Eugene Schuller manufactures the first commercial hair color and calls his company "The French Harmless Hair Dye Co." Within a year, he wisely changes the name to L'Oreal.

1914—Max Factor gets his start providing wigs to actors in Hollywood westerns, on condition his sons are given parts as extras.

1920s—First home hairdryer developed in Germany. It was made of steel with a wooden handle.

1964—Hip girls throw away their curlers and plug in an iron to straighten their hair.

1975—Rastafarian reggae king Bob Marley makes dreadlocks drop-dead natty; Number "10" Bo Derek wears corn rows with beads to the beach.

1996—Buzz cuts are *hot*, giving thin-haired men a shot at a social life.

EAST AND WEST AGREE

Japanese women in the 17th century arranged their hair in elaborate coiffures swept up with ornamental combs and pins and ribbons, revealing the nape of the neck, which men thought erotic. Interestingly, the 1890s "Gibson Girl" had her hair combed up and over a pad frame in a pompadour similar to a geisha's. In Japan today, geishas still sweep up their hair in the celebrated hairdo.

WIGGED OUT

Although real hair rarely stopped being combed and dyed and dusted and styled for fashion, in some eras it has been the wig that dominated time, money and style.

Egyptian noblemen and noblewomen wore black wigs for special ceremonies held under the hot sun. Their own hair was cropped short or shaved off. Their wigs were complicated affairs, comprised of many tight small braids adorned with ivory hairpins, fresh flowers or gold ornaments, and scented with perfume. A mixture made of warm beeswax and resin glued the curls and braids to a

CARNAVALET

mesh cap. Egyptian wigs and hair extensions were constructed out of horsehair, palm leaves, lamb's wool and straw. The wigmakers, who were barbers, too, were literally slaves to style.

In ancient Rome, aristocratic women sometimes wore blonde wigs made from hair shorn from their fair-haired Teutonic slaves.

Elizabeth I is said to have owned eighty wigs in different colors and styles. Wigs became a necessity as her hairline receded along with her youth; her hair loss had been accelerated by her fondness for lead-based makeup. Her servants could change the hue of any wig by dusting it with violet, white or "blonde" powder before decorating it with jewels, feathers and fancy hairpins.

Aristocratic gents joined the ladies in the wig wars that started in 1661 when Louis XIV of France began losing his hair at age twenty-three. On with the wig or one didn't show his or her head in polite society. Louis employed 48 wigmakers at court.

A century later, in 1769, French baker Legros de Rumigny became a court hairdresser and opened the first hairdressing school, *Academie de Coiffure*, to train others to serve nobles properly.

But the women still kept men on their toes; in fact, many men needed a ladder to pat the top of ladies' heads. The Marie Antoinette wig was a fantastic piece of architecture. The queen literally raised the wig to new heights after her hair fell out, following the birth of her first child in 1774. She favored real-hair wigs built into her own hair over wire

CARNAVALET

CARNAVALET

frames stuffed with horsehair pads, cotton wool, shreds of rope and cow's tail. Peddlers roamed the countryside buying hair from the poor and heirs of the dead. Ten human heads were needed to yield enough hair for one wig. *Voilà*—the term "bigwig" was born.

The enormous construction was held together with pins and gobs of pomade, and powdered with ground starch. Some wigs rose three feet in the air and had springs to adjust their height. Wig designers went crazy decorating them with ribbons, jewels and even little garden scenes, stuffed birds and miniature ships. A good wig had a nine-week lifetime. When not in use, the wigs were paradise for lice and other vermin. To keep them out, the hairy roach motels were smoothed down with lard and covered with rat-resistant wire cages.

By the 18th century, each profession had its own style of wig.

Fashionable men sent their wigs out to the barber on Saturday to be brushed and curled in time to be worn that night. Placing a wig on a head was no mean feat. First, a valet positioned it on the head; next, he draped his master's fine clothing with sheeting and covered his face with a paper mask. Only then could the bountiful wig be powdered. All this action took place in an appropriately named space: the "powder room." The powder room traveled with the privileged few to colonial America.

Mere strivers had to content themselves with sad, dirty secondhand wigs; if they thought to re-powder them, the white mist probably settled on everything else they owned. Wigs were so expensive for ordinary souls that they were bequeathed in wills.

Less Is Not More

Baldness marks the man, but only rarely favorably, for reasons already made clear. But what to do about it?

Over the centuries, recipes have been jotted down for magic potions to promote hair growth by mixing roots, snake parts, herbs and oils. Today's balding men can buy bottled formulas, but a better head through chemistry remains elusive. Men continue to scratch their bald heads and worry.

According to one study, two-thirds of balding men spend time looking in the mirror at what's left of their hair, and they ruefully touch their heads and talk about their baldness. In another study, both men and women looked at pictures of bald men and men with full heads of hair; both genders found the bald men less socially acceptable, less attractive physically and less likely to be successful. No wonder more men are going for cornrow punch grafts and other surgical hair-transplant techniques.

Sen. William Proxmire has made it acceptable for *real* men to have hair transplants. These days, follicle-challenged movie stars and rock artists are particularly likely to go for drastic remedies. Burt Reynolds, Michael Keaton, Billy Crystal, Nicolas Cage and Stacy Keach are among those rumored to have had transplants or have spent small fortunes on "rugs." For them, the cost of vanity is a legitimate tax deduction.

Nicolas Cage and other celebs are rumored to have more hair than Nature gave them.

To Dye For

Coloring hair sends all kinds of cues. A few years ago, teenagers went in for neon independence statements by dying strips of their hair hot pink, turquoise and glow-in-the-dark green. Their color choices were not as original as they thought. Ancient Greek women dyed their hair red or blue, then dusted it with gold or red powders.

The original hair dye, henna, was used in the city of Ur. Henna and walnut rinses kept citizens' dark hair shiny and gave it highlights from rust to purple.

As for the finishing touch—not all natural conditioners are appealing. One antique hair gel recipe calls for swallow droppings and lizard tallow. A test perhaps of how badly a woman wanted soft hair.

The jury is still out on whether blondes throughout time have had more fun. The association of blondness with loose women goes far back in Mediterranean history. But that didn't stop Greek women, in about 300 B.C., from lightening their hair with saffron.

To achieve the desired "Titian red," that delicious strawberry blond favored by the painter, Renaissance women spent hours mixing black sulfur, alum and honey and spreading it on their long tresses, which they then dried in the sun. If they didn't develop scalp scabs or lose half their hair, they were the envy of their neighbors.

The leap from there to the Jersey shore, where adolescent girls sit with their hair dripping in lemon juice, undergoing a natural bleach job, is shorter than you think.

For thrifty types, the formulas come in bottles. For movie stars—from Marilyn Monroe to Nicole Kidman and Gwyneth Paltrow—and legions of others with spare cash, blondeness is hand-mixed and applied by specialists known as colorists. The salon process has two steps: a colorist strips the natural hue from a client's tresses, then paints them with the new tone. Drips from the stripping chemicals may burn the scalp, although gentler formulas have ensured that bottle blondes suffer less than they did in Monroe's day.

The other color found less often in nature than some admit to is red or dark auburn, a color typified by Raquel Welch in her prime. Her crowning glory, of course, was just the finishing touch on this actress, who mapped out her own place in the beauty wars. Of Welch, a *Time* writer said, "She is the nubile savage crying out to be bashed on the skull and dragged to some lair by her wild auburn mane."

Madonna shares her hair space with no one. She has been every color—for whatever role she's vamping. But she will enter the Hair Color Hall of Fame as the girl who made it fashionable to let your roots show.

Chic to her roots: the modern Madonna

BLUE RIBBON BRAGGART #3

"I'm not offended by all the dumb blonde jokes because I'm not dumb and I'm not blonde."—DOLLY PARTON

Of Low and High Brows

Nature invented eyebrows to protect eyes from sweat and dust. Many, however, have found them unnecessary. Roman women kept in style 2500 years ago by removing them with iron razors, pumice stones, homemade depilatories and primitive tweezers. The practice of shaving off eyebrows also marked the Middle Ages. Fashionable women in Chaucer's time plucked them out completely. The Mbaya tribe of the Amazon removes their brows, too, and calls white men "ostrich brothers."

Aesthetically, eyebrows act as ornamental awnings, drawing attention to the windows—our eyes. The Greeks appreciated this enough to make false eyebrows out of dyed goat's hair. One heir to the Greek tradition was Groucho Marx, who attached furry bushes above his eyes to give greater expression to his face as he delivered one-liners.

Marlene Dietrich's eyebrows were straight from the pencil—drawn very thin and long. In 1939, Helena Rubinstein wrote in *The Art of Feminine Beauty*, "I am happy that the fad of plucking, shaving and otherwise slenderizing the eyebrows is far less popular than it has been in the past. I have steadily preached against overdoing it." Of course, she was also promoting her castor oil eyebrow cream.

The look of celebrity brows today can be bought with an eyebrow stencil kit. Just pick your model: A rounded shape softens the features of Gwyneth Paltrow and Julia Roberts; angled brows copied from Demi Moore and Uma Thurman will lend youth to your visage (and people won't know why); flat shapes are perfect for those with long faces like Brooke Shields and Julia Ormond.

Final Take

"I go into that shop and they're so great
looking, and I'm doin' their hair and
they feel so good and they smell great and
that's it. It makes my day. It makes me
feel like I'm going to live forever."
—George (WARREN BEATTY) to Jill
(GOLDIE HAWN), *Shampoo* (Columbia
Pictures), 1975

CHAPTER FOUR

BODY

SCULPTURE

No culture is immune from drastic rituals to attract the opposite sex, to ward off evil spirits or to uphold social status. Altering the shape of our skull, lips, nose and ears or sculpting the body to meet an ideal standard may seem odd to outsiders, but in the society where it happens it represents beauty, and enduring the attendant discomfort is a sign of honor. Pain is usually temporary while ostracism can last forever.

The Cutting Edge

Finally, when the diets don't work, cosmetics don't cover and the zipper won't slide over the flesh mountain, it's time for plastic surgery. Cosmetic surgery these days includes face and neck lifts, eyelids, laser resurfacing, nose jobs, tummy tucks, liposuction, breast augmentation, and buttock lifts. Any of these procedures is increasing-

Ideal Self Image One: female version
Ideal Self Image Two: male version

ly socially acceptable, and yet people still tend to go on vacation or into hibernation right after.

Who would think that women who are required by law to cover their hair and conceal their female shape in loose robes would dare expose a surgical bandage on the face? In some Iranian circles, the bandage is worn like a war medal to let everyone know you have money to buy beauty. Beauty has always been integral to Persian culture. As one proverb tells us: "Kill me, but make me beautiful." Pretty strong stuff.

Last year, *The New York Times* reported that a "rail thin," 30-year-old Iranian, Lili Moghimi, had already had two nose jobs and fingernail implants, as well as having her eyebrows tattooed to make them look darker.

In Morocco, surgical blades showed up in Mohammed VI's court. An American plastic surgeon was summoned with his team of nurses and anesthesiologists to Rabat. Escorted directly from the plane to the Royal Palace, he performed facelifts and scar touch-ups on the king's harem, in a state-of-the-art palace hospital. These women patiently awaited their turns to go under the knife, wearing peignoirs and embroidered slippers. Very civilized.

Cosmetic surgery grew out of reconstructive surgery, which was practiced in India as far back as the sixth century B.C. Two common surgeries performed then repaired clipped ears and dam-

When the veil is dropped: Who can say whether wealthy Islamic women go under the knife for their girlfriends or their husbands? Cosmetic surgery could be Wife #1's weapon against Wives # 2, 3 and 4.

Nose Job Patient: An Italian nobleman in recovery over 400 years ago.

aged noses with skin patches from the cheek. Mutilated noses were common because nasal amputation was a punishment for adultery. Repair surgeries were performed by a caste of potters; presumably a man who could sculpt a clay pot could also mold a new nose.

Medieval Italian aristocrats tended to solve dueling injuries to their noses with reconstructive surgery. The flesh used in the repair might come from a serf, persuaded or coerced into trading skin for his freedom.

One account of a 16th-century nose job describes the quick thinking of a Calabrian military surgeon at an army camp in Africa, where one day a 21-year-old Spaniard, Andres Gutiero, got into a fight with another soldier. In a stroke, the soldier cut off Gutiero's nose, which fell to the ground. The doctor, who had witnessed the injury, impulsively picked up the nose, which was full of sand. The enterprising surgeon urinated on the nose to clean it and sewed it back on the poor Spaniard. The surgeon bandaged his handiwork, thinking for sure it would rot. But eight days later, when the bandage was removed, the patient was healthy and his nose was healing nicely.

Gaspare Tagliacozzi (1545-1599) is the first man known to have specialized in plastic surgery. His success led, as it would today, to a rush of clients. Tagliacozzi set up a hospital in his enormous Bologna house. Over the entrance door was a large golden snout with these words

"DE CURTURUM CHIRUGIA" FROM LIFE OF G. TAGLIACOZZI, VENICE, 1597, COURTESY OF THE NEW YORK ACADEMY OF MEDICINE

from Ovid written underneath: "Every lover is a soldier and his camp is Cupid."

The rich and nose-unhappy of Europe flocked to his door. A series of regional wars assured Tagliacozzi of a steady supply of clients. The surgeon also ensured a monopoly by gaining a patent granting him the exclusive right to manufacture noses from a flap of skin sliced from a patient's arm. Furthermore, the celebrated surgeon guaranteed clients that their recon-

U.S. PATENT OFFICE, 1922

INVENTIONS OF DESIRE

In 1892, George Burwell, a Boston chemist, advertised a thick belt made of medicated flannel and covered in silk, which carried 100 electrical-charged magnets in order to disintegrate fat: "Any size made to order for gentlemen and ladies!" The price must have given a jolt to buyers, who coughed up between $5 and $15 dollars for the obesity belt, depending on the size.

In June 1924, long before the pouty-lip look was achieved with collagen shots, the "Cupid's Bow Shaper" was patented to make a depression in the middle of the upper lip and reshape it into a heart.

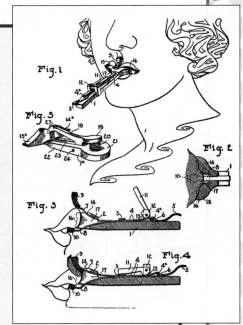

Gadget for shaping a Cupid's-bow lip.

structed noses would be capable of inhaling snuff and sneezing.

Tagliacozzi was not without artistry and he charged accordingly. If a patient wanted an elegant Roman nose the price was high, but an ordinary, short nose was a relative bargain.

Only Half the World Knows for Sure

Did she? Did he? Current celebrities have made it easier for mere mortals to admit an eyelift or some chin work, or pinches and tucks, drainage or amplification on the body. Cosmetic surgery has come out of the closet and onto TV talk shows.

Marilyn Monroe, however, went under the knife in the days when stars were still secretive about self-improvement. The story goes that she decided on surgery, in 1949, after overhearing herself described as a "chinless wonder." Monroe went on to have a slight imperfection in her nose fixed, and sponge implants and silicone injections in her breasts, but she viewed lights and cameras as unforgiving. "When my looks start to go, so will most of my fans," she lamented.

Surprise! The flawless face of French beauty Catherine Deneuve is rumored held together with gold mesh inserted under her skin. It sounds more like a jealous dig at her extreme beauty.

The verdict is black and white on Michael Jackson. Before and after photos aren't even close. Jackson has used surgery to challenge his own DNA. The African-American teen disappeared two decades ago and turned into a cream-skinned man with high cheekbones and a narrow nose. In the course of multiple operations, his chin even acquired a Clint Eastwood cleft.

One of the 90s' bigger renovation jobs may have been on Roseanne Barr. Face lift, nose job, breast reduction, liposuction and tummy tuck. For stunning results, however, few public personalities equal Cher, who once confessed, "I am the equivalent of a counterfeit $25 dollar bill." She claims, however, that only her nose and her breasts have been altered by surgeons.

Only their surgeons know for sure (left to right): Catherine Deneuve, Michael Jackson, and Cher.

Needle Point Beauty

When the knife gets too expensive the needle will do. Dermatologists are now the new best friends of the worried with wrinkles. Shots of collagen (protein extracted from cows) or botox (a purified drug produced from bacteria) are the prickly "hot" cures. Injections un-wrinkle foreheads and brows, and diminish crow's feet by pumping up the skin beneath the creases and, in the case of botox, paralyzing nerves. Age lines disappear. At least, for four to six months.

The Agony and The Ecstasy

Not every culture finds smooth skin appealing. In parts of Africa, the person who is ornately scarred is one to be respected for courage or beauty. The art of scarring long defined the ideal person in parts of the Sudan, Nigeria and Ethiopia.

At puberty, Karo girls of Ethiopia endured a painful passage into adulthood. Razor-like cuts were made into their abdomens and ashes were rubbed into the wounds, which made them heal in a raised pattern. The designs resembled those we admire on African textiles or woodcuts.

Heads Up

A baby's soft head made it a good vehicle for reshaping by several peoples. Natives of the Pacific Northwest bound an infant's head between two boards to elongate it. Mothers of the Hopi and Navajo tribes bound their babies' heads into a cone-shape, which identified them as free men and women.

The heads of Inca infants of noble birth were shaped into a point to distinguish them from commoners.

The Mangbetu people of northeastern Congo tightly circled the heads of their infants with fine threads; adults wrapped their own heads to keep the elongated look, accentuated by headdresses on special occasions.

During the 19th century, head shaping was still practiced in the French provinces. A French Jesuit, Father Josset, believed that by shaping the head one could shape the child's future vocation and talents. He advised mothers to bind their infants' heads so that "their offspring might in due time produce great orators."

Heads are malleable in the interests of distinction and beauty.

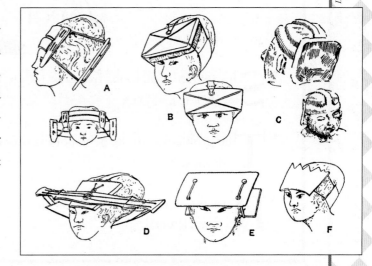

Deformaciones Internacionales by Adolpho Dembo and J. Imbelloni, Buenos Aires

When Europeans first saw the Padaung women of southeast Asia, they called them "the giraffe women" because of their elongated necks (some a foot long), ringed in close-fitting brass bangles. Long, stiff necks delineated feminine beauty; the rings signified wealth. Girls as young as five had their necks ringed to stretch them; more bangles were added until a girl married. The true beauty might wear 30 heavy necklaces.

Padaung women necessarily held their heads high; one consequence of neck ringing was they could not look down. An adulterous woman was stripped of her bangles. The penalty was more than visual; she'd likely have trouble breathing because her unsupported neck was without muscle tone.

LAUGH LINES

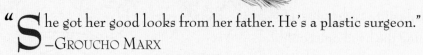

"She got her good looks from her father. He's a plastic surgeon."
    —GROUCHO MARX

"The problem with the gene pool is that there is no lifeguard."
    —UNKNOWN WIT

"Darwin would be happy to know that my face is in a constant state of evolution."
    —JOAN RIVERS

Body Piercing

Nose piercing isn't new.

Four thousand years ago in Iraq and Iran, men and women pierced their ears and hung golden loops through them. The earrings were thought to repel the demon; and no doubt looked pretty good too. Ear piercing is one of the more usual beauty enhancements on earth; it also has the plus of being a good way to display valuables. Children have pierced ears almost as often as adults. One sweet twist is in Borneo, where, when a child reaches puberty, his mother and father each pierce one of his earlobes to symbolize that he is *still* dependent on them.

Two decades ago in New York, a nine-year-old girl walked into a Chinese laundry with her mother, proudly showing off her newly pierced ears. An elderly Chinaman (perhaps 80 years old) grinned at the girl and said, " Me too," whereupon he showed her *his* single pierced earlobe. The old man's son explained that it had been a custom in Imperial China to pierce one ear of a precious first-born son to protect the boy. It was necessary to fool the gods into thinking he was merely a girl, lest they take him away.

Nose piercing, while a new trend for Western teenagers, is a longstanding custom in India, Pakistan, Alaska and many other places. Until recent decades, Potok tribesmen in Africa favored leaf-shaped nose pendants. A woman, however, wore a small, round bone plug pierced in below her lower lip. In other tribes, such a face adornment was a male accessory, attached above the lip.

The Aztec and Maya drew a cord of thorns through the tongue as a form of sacrifice. The mutilated tongue empowered them to communicate with the gods.

Long Lobes, Platform Lips

Once upon a time, a girl of the Nandi tribe in Africa had the bottom of her earlobe stretched by a series of heavy elephant-hair loops until the lobe itself transformed into a circle earring. Heavy metal hoops have been used to achieve this in more recent times.

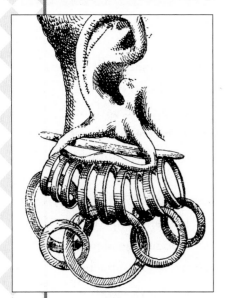

Fortunately, the earlobe has very few nerve ends and little feeling. But the pressure on a young girl whose ears were being stretched must have given her quite a headache.

Certain African tribes have favored super-size lips over artistic, long ears. Fat lips don't mean you've lost the fight. They show that you've won. Some anthropologists believe exaggerated lip extensions started as a ploy to deter slave traders from taking women away from the tribe. Who would want them with their distorted lips? Other evidence points to large lips being associated with belief in sacred animals. For whatever reason, extended lips became a tribal signifier and a mark of beauty.

In the mid-1900s in Chad, the Sara women, commonly known as Ubangi, still used ceramic saucers to drag down their lower lips. Meanwhile, the Kichepo women of southeast Sudan extended their lips with huge wedge-shaped plates into a shape reminiscent of the broadbill bird.

In Ethiopia, the Mursi tribe cuts a hole into the lower lip of a girl at puberty. A small plate is inserted, replaced by progressively larger ones until the lower lip is about the size of a teacup saucer. The larger the lip, the higher the price the girl will fetch on the marriage market. In 2000, one woman commanded 50 head of cattle as her bridal price.

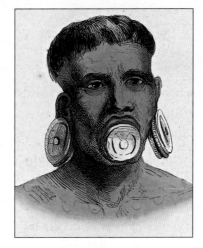
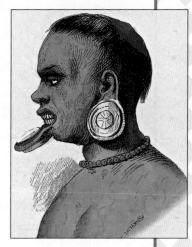

One needs a "stiff upper lip" to achieve the large lower lip style favored by some Central Africans.

Blue Ribbon Braggart # 4

"I've always had such a good physique and such intense charm that it's difficult to be true to myself."
—Lawrence Durrell

PRIDE AND PAIN

A t first glance, cone heads, stretched necks and other artificially achieved body extremes may seem a circus of deformities, deserving of pity or laughter but not sympathetic identification. But why not? *Every culture*, ours included, has its beauty fetishes. And there are many on earth who'd be stupefied to learn that rich Americans suction off fat from their bodies.

After the pain comes the healing. One woman, who traveled to a plastic surgeon out of state, exulted, "I got a chin implant and frequent flyer miles, too."

FINAL TAKE

"No matter what a woman does, a younger woman will always walk into the room."
–Comment made to Barbara Sawyer (ELIZABETH TAYLOR), *Ash Wednesday* (Paramount), 1973

CHAPTER FIVE

FOUNDATION

STATEMENTS

David by Michelangelo.

Art celebrates nudity. We gaze in admiration at Michelangelo's *David* and wonder where the plastic surgeon is who could do that for flesh and blood men. Nudity in real life is more complicated. The fig leaf signifies volumes. From the beginning, the lingerie industry has had as much to do with sin as with support.

Natural cover-ups have been the fashion in many places east and west of Eden. Men and women in the tropics have shielded their intimate parts with grasses, raffia or gourds (organic jock straps), from Ambryn Island in the western Pacific to the Amazon basin. But in many warm places, bosoms went uncovered. A female's bare breasts were part of her maternal role, not a provocative come-on.

Except when fashion dictated otherwise. In Minoan Crete, women wore laced corsets that supported breasts but left them bare. There were periods when small or diminished-looking breasts were a preferred standard of beauty and even considered an asset to saving the soul. Ancient Greek women banded down their breasts with leather straps.

The Greeks were also leaders in the cultural development of the chastity belt, a woolly girdle fastened with a complicated knot. Folklore claims that a Circassian custom was to provide girls between seven and eight years old with broad leather girdles that were tightly knotted around the waist and not removed until marriage seven years later. On the girl's

This Medieval portrait of a young man consulting a physician illustrates drawers over stockings.

wedding night, the groom cut the knot with a sharp dagger.

In general, the longer and heavier a culture's traditional clothing, the less likely it is that underwear lies beneath. The weighty kimono pressed against bare skin. The classic long Arabic robe cloaks the body so effectively usually no undergarments are required. But men in short skirts can catch a chill from the glare of a voyeur or a winter draft, so most Scotsmen wore loincloths under their kilts.

Underwear, as we know it, became chic in Europe during the Middle Ages, when nobility traded up from sheepskins to more artful apparel. Linen underskirts and smocks helped prolong the lives of women's expensive, fussy gowns and men's elaborate tunic tops. These linen garments next to the skin were buffers against the moisture and odor of infrequently washed bodies. It literally became a class distinction to be able to change underwear. Undergarments of the rich were laundered by servants who scrubbed them in a tub of cold water, then laid them out on the grass or hedge to dry in the sun. That could take days.

Not only did foundation wear marginally stem the stench about the castle; it kept its aristocratic wearers warmer as they stepped away from the fire. Underclothing also had the advantage of protecting them from the abrasive silver and gold metal threads woven into their embroidered and sometimes jewel-studded velvets and brocades.

What's Underneath? A loincloth—sometimes.

BLUE RIBBON BRAGGART #5

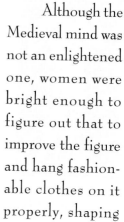

"I thank God I am imbued with such qualities that if I were turned out of the realm in my petticoat I would be able to live in any place in Christendom." —ELIZABETH I

Although the Medieval mind was not an enlightened one, women were bright enough to figure out that to improve the figure and hang fashionable clothes on it properly, shaping had to be done. And people long ago realized that, to flatten the stomach, push up the boobs and slenderize the waist, someone had to pull strings. With enough pressure brought to bear, the idealized female shape was only a strong tug away. There may have been some mavericks who tossed away the stays of fashion's dictates, but they did not prevail. Glamour with its concomitant pain ruled. Here we review some underpinnings that have pinched, pulled, flattened, padded or seductively exposed the body.

PULLING THE STRINGS

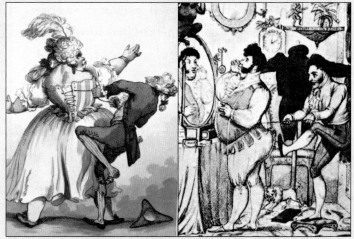

FAB ABS

Ancient Persians invented the "regulation girdle." One of the king's male officials bore the title of "chief holder of the girdle." His job was to measure the ladies in the harem to see that they all fit the one size deemed perfect by the king. If a lady had outgrown the girdle, she was put on a diet. If she didn't fill up the girdle, she was fattened like a Strasbourg goose.

Shockingly few improvements were made in girdle design before the mid-20th century. Without the assistance of the stiff, rubber case that cocooned a woman from waist to mid-thigh, or the heavily boned, full-torso foundation made of sturdy fabric, most fashion-conscious women couldn't slide into the slim skirts and dresses of the 1930s, 40s and early 50s. Even those truly thin enough for sheath dresses needed to hold up their stockings and keep down backside wiggling. ("Nice girls don't jiggle," said the proper young co-eds of the era.) A Merry Widow (a decorative waist-nipping corselet with dangling garters) or a garter belt (a circle of lightweight fabric or ribbon, hooked around the waist, with swinging garters) might keep hose from falling down, but only the real girdle loaned its super firmness to both tummy and tail. Was it uncomfortable? If you're not in a position to remember, ask your mother or grandmother what life as a sausage felt like.

In 1959, women began breathing easier, thanks to Du Pont. Lingerie manufacturers began offering lighter girdles made of spandex, the elastic fabric engineered by German chemists back in 1937. Spandex could be stretched out five times its length and then snap back to its original size. The new-style girdles offered more mobility than the old but no girdle is fun—which is why panty hose, essentially a lighter sausage casing, or stockings with elasticized tops or no hose at all are what the hard-of-body or loose-at-heart prefer.

Of Chain Mail and Corsets

In the 12th century, knights in shining armor and their ladies shared the same couturier: the local armor-maker or blacksmith. The female garment, a sleeveless affair worn over her gown, was constructed of leather, "boned" with iron fillets and laced tightly. But while the gentleman needed only to wear his rig during war (more frequent than not) or for the odd peacetime joust, some ladies of the court were dressed in their metal cages from sunrise to well past sunset every day. Comfy.

Well into the 16th century, blacksmiths banged out the iron strips for stays that literally turned women into walking metal mannequins *under* or as part of their dress bodices, although corsets stiffened with stays of wood, whalebone, ivory and leather had their proponents through much of the long, crushing corset era.

The mission of the corset, past and present, is to narrow the waistline and mash down the midriff by sheer *push*, which in turn shoves up the bust. When low necklines rule and corset strings are pulled with the right calculation, the bust spills up and out. All this compression can make its mark on a woman. The brilliant pink and red impressions that whalebone left on a woman's skin were the least of it. Strong tugs on a corset's string could break a woman's ribs. It happened to Nicole Kidman while she was being fitted for her courtesan costume on the set of *Moulin Rouge*. If a lady of fashion spoke with a breathy voice, it was possibly because of her limited air intake. A really effective Victorian corset could and did displace internal organs.

Lingerie advertising in Victorian England was only slightly coy about the torture inherent in distorting one's shape with stays: "Elegance Before Comfort," boasted one corset-maker.

Even hundreds of years ago, a few physicians expressed alarm. One 17th-century doctor

A Perfect Health Corset, Superior to all Others.

FERRIS'

warned that "girls ought to be wiser. They lock themselves in a jail of irons and stays, but they open the door wide to consumption."

Sir Erasmus Wilson (1809-1884), President of the Royal College of Surgeons, sighed, "It is a small wonder that fashionable women and working girls who are foolish enough to follow their bad example, feel languid, oppressed, and low-spirited . . . tight-lacing in time induces a feeling of hypochondria which leads to confirmed illness." Condemned by doctors, encouraged by fashionable schools and regarded by mothers as a necessity for future social success, the corset continued its immense popularity.

Even little girls wore tiny corsets to achieve the idealized female body. Early 19th century child-beauty contests at festivals awarded little girls prizes for the smallest waist or the flattest back. The transition from swaddling to binding was not that great; tiny girls were tucked securely into woolly or stiff cotton corsets. By the time they were nine years old they were ready for the real thing, corsets just like Mama's, reinforced with bones, steel and stiff cording. The hourglass silhouette corset looked nothing like the body of the child who wore it. But the heavy lacing accomplished two things: an 18-inch waist by the early teens and straitlaced behavior for ten-year-olds.

The corset effectively stopped polite middle-class girls from climbing, hopping, leaping or standing on one leg. This was extremely upsetting to Charles Darwin's granddaughters, who grew up at the end of the 19th century. In her 1952 memoir, Gwen Ravera remembered impetuously stripping off her own childhood corset while her sister "ran round and round the nursery screaming with rage."

Victorian little girls played with dolls with nipped in waists and broad hips, the Barbies of the day. The dolls, too, had corsets in their wardrobes.

Some young 19th-century Englishwomen were so proud of the narrow waists they achieved with the help of corsets, they wore dog collars for belts. It could be an urban legend, but it's said that more than one husband kept the collar that his wife wore before she became a matron to remind himself of her once tiny waist.

It took World War I to free some women from their unyielding undergarments. The respected Washington socialite and activist, Mrs. Nicholas Longworth, née Alice Roosevelt, (1884-1980), led the campaign to convince women to surrender their steel stays for the war effort. The War Board re-ported, "American women's sacrifice of their stays during the first World War released 28,000 tons of steel—enough to build two battleships."

THE WET LOOK

Getting a cold for the sake of fashion goes back at least to the early 1800s, when it was the French fad for ladies to dampen their muslin Empire gowns, in all seasons, so that they would cling to their bodies.

A Naughty Nineties burlesque girl.

THE CASE FOR CODPIECES

The codpiece is not a portion of fish, although it could be fishy looking if overly padded. To understand the codpiece, one needs to consider the plight of men in tights. Close-fitting hosiery and short tunics were all the rage in 15th-century Europe. But in an age before Lycra, the short tunics created certain challenges for the man who would be stylishly attired. There were issues of support, of revealing desire, of utmost vulnerability.

Protection was the number one concern of the soldier

DRAG QUEEN

While women happily displayed their cleavage, with the aid of tight corsets and pads, convention forced them to keep even the shapeliest of legs hidden. Vivacious Elizabeth of Russia, who ascended the throne in 1741, and happened to have a pair of great-looking gams, couldn't abide the restraint. So the *tsarina* devised a Winter Palace entertainment to show off her legs: the transvestite ball. Men dressed as women and women as men. Although some of her hundreds of guests must have been uncomfortable, the *tsarina's* short tunic and tights beautifully displayed her well-turned legs and she held the room in fascination.

whose upper torso was shielded in mail or more solid metal but who might find his family jewels at risk in battle. For him, the armorer had devised a protective covering called the codpiece. It was a metal shield roundly shaped to fit over the groin and ingeniously hinged to the torso armor. The hinge allowed for a quick response to natural urges.

Clever tailors adapted this concept for men in civilian roles. The burgher's codpiece was a bag of stiff leather or heavy cloth, sometimes stuffed with protective straw. Exteriors of some dress-up codpieces were gem-studded. The bag was laced to the man's stockings, which were made up of two separate leg pieces pulled up to the waist and attached to his tunic from within. Peasants wore codpieces well into the 17th century, even after breeches were the norm; they were secured with leather lacing but naked of decorative detail.

For the Knight in Shining Armor: Note the codpiece.

What Was Hip: No slithering through narrow doorways in a dress draped over a farthingale, hoop or pannier.

HIPPY DAYS

A Renaissance invention, called the farthingale, exaggerated the hipline to the fashonable largeness that reigned for four centuries, except for a brief collapse during the Napoleonic era. The late 15th-century Spanish farthingale was a bell-shaped under-structure, made of pliant willow twigs or cane or as much as fifty yards of whalebone.

The 16th-century French farthingale was an even more generous hip-enhancer. It was like wearing a Hoola Hoop under a dress. Wood or whalebone was bent into a succession of wheel shapes and attached to a canvas petticoat. The fabric fell straight down on the sides of the "drum," allowing ladies to parade in a profusion of velvet and silk. But this architectural foundation made it difficult to cozy up to a lover, a quality that seemingly suited England's Virgin Queen. Elizabeth, whose fashion collection included over one thousand dresses, loved the farthingale. She recognized that her *expansive*, highly decorated gowns beautifully projected her image of power.

Pots and Panniers

In the late-17th century, the farthingale was replaced by a foundation that made walking between rooms almost impossible. Called a pannier, it made waists appear yet smaller and hips titanic. Constructed of cane, metal or wood latticework and covered in linen, this skirt support, which looked like two upside-down baskets, was attached to each hip with strong strings around the waist. Super-wide petticoats and dresses were draped over the bulk; by the mid-18th century, a woman's hips might measure as much as 18 feet across, wide enough to serve pots of tea on each hip. (An enterprising 18th-century inventor created a collapsible mechanism to allow passage through a doorway, and Louis XV chairs, with their cutaway arms, were designed to accommodate the panniers.)

In a London magazine issue of 1751, an anonymous observer noted, "Ladies have found some inconvenience surely in the circular hoop because they have changed it to that extensive oblong form . . . I have been in a moderate large room, where there have been *but* two ladies, who had not space enough to move."

More Hoopla

Walking in a cage of steel wire or worked wood made it difficult to tiptoe over puddles (not everyone had Sir Walter Raleigh at her side) or get a good whack at the ball during a round of croquet. By the 1830s, numerous petticoats (as many as three or four) had replaced the more structured farthingales and panniers, but they were no walk in the park, either. The mid-19th century invention of the hoop, strengthened with metal or bone, relieved women of wearing weighty layers of starched crinolines. Now a woman could look fashionably wide-hipped by fitting into just one giant hoop made of boned rings (the more rings the rounder the hoop) and *one* plain flannel or cotton petticoat for warmth under her dress. The bell-shaped hoop held nine concentric rings for a day dress and as many as 18 for an evening ball gown.

By the late 1850s, heavy whalebone rings had been replaced by lighter watch-spring wire. In 1860, the world of fashion briefly witnessed the fad of inflatable hoops, blown up by a small foot pump.

Bum Wraps

One bump on the fashion road was a backward design that trailed behind a woman: the bustle. This bulge on the backside began as a soft pad, more or less held in place by ties around the woman's waist. As early as the 14th century, women were exaggerating the rear view by sewing foxtails under the backs of their heavy skirts.

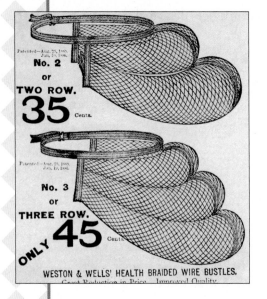

Prominent Rear View: The wire-mesh bustle helped achieve the prized look of the late 19th century.

The "bum roll," whose popularity peaked early in the 17th century, was not a fanny enhancer despite its name. Rather, it was a fabric donut that provided a lift to heavy skirts on informal occasions when the farthingale was not *de rigueur*. Ladies' maids fashioned the bum roll by stuffing cotton wool or cork into a linen casing. This inner-tube underwear gave women rounded hips and behinds, and bulging stomachs, but at least they looked like sweet plump sausages all the way around.

The backside became a fashion focus again at the end of the 19th century when big and small bustles supported dresses and skirts with fancy folds, bows and other doodads concentrated on the target area. The best bustles were fabric-covered tubes of wire coils or whalebone sticks. A bustle was attached to a lady's waist by a thin cloth waistband.

Women who wanted to remain standing had no problems with this back bulge, but to sit down required shifting the bustle to one side and perching gently on a seat.

Bum Wrap: The padded hip donut added considerable presence, as illustrated in this mocking 17th-century engraving.

LARGE DETAIL COPIED FROM WORK BY MAARTEN DE VOS.

Bien tost les ferayie rondes & alaigres.
Compt proper dierkens wilt op dese fatsoene letten
Ick sal v mager billen wat int ronde
setten

Vn cachenfant come les
Couste qu'il couste . le
Ick moet een cac
Mij en rock wa

"Brevity is the soul of lingerie."
—Dorothy Parker

ETCHING BY LEWIS MARK, CIRCA 1800

Spindleshanks: For the poor fellow without shapely calves to slip into stockings, there was padded help.

Falsies for Guys

The male stocking was not a flash in the fashion pan. We've seen how the codpiece addressed the difficulties of men in tights with short tops. But even after men pulled ornate balloon shorts or Capri pants over their hosiery, the calf remained outlined. Frankly, not all guys could face the world without some help.

Stuffing was an answer for men without shapely, muscular calves. It is impossible to say how long men had been padding their tights to develop more pronounced leg muscles, though 17th-century French actors, like Molière and his troupe, used this leg-enhancing device. But by the early 19th century, when white silk stockings were still required of officers and gentlemen, false calves were available for purchase.

We get an inside story from the memoirs of one French army officer, Coignet. In 1809, Coignet entered Paris in Napoleon's army. Soon, the provincial was promoted to sergeant, and with this rank came new social obligations. He had to learn to write and he had to wear white silk stockings. Although the ladies apparently considered young Coignet to have a handsome face, he was keenly aware that he lacked pronounced calves and sought to remedy this by wearing budget-breaking falsies hidden under his hose.

One night, his commander invited him to a banquet where he met a beautiful, sophisticated lady who later called him to her bedchamber. Coignet managed to take off his fake calves and smuggle them under his pillow on her magnificent bed. Speed, fear of being caught, or darkness must have hindered his efforts to get dressed again when it was time to go, because when Coignet appeared back in his barracks, his friends noticed lumps in his stocking and accused him of wearing falsies. He immediately took them off and threw them in the fire, "From now on it's spindle shanks for me," Coignet decided. Calf pads remained part of other men's wardrobes for several decades.

I See London, I See France . . .

It was not until the early 1800s that chic ladies began wearing drawers or pantaloons under their dresses: wide loose pants made of fine linen, handkerchief cotton and sometimes even silk, which were gathered at the ankles with ruffles.

Pantaloons could be considered the first aerobic wear, as they were excellent for sporty women. Thirty years before most ladies stocked them, they were worn by skaters (particularly the Dutch), dancers, little girls who romped on the lawn and bigger girls who did gymnastics. Some

The Bloomer Costume

CURRIER & IVES

society women found pantaloons "absolutely essential" in the country, according to a French journal of 1824, as security against unexpected falls while riding.

Within a decade, *pantalettes* or pantaloons were under many fashionable skirts; when, in mid-century, the hoop supplanted layers of crinoline, allowing indecent exposure at unexpected moments, propriety absolutely demanded that a woman cover her lower parts. But wearing pantaloons as modest underwear was quite a different matter from wearing pants for outerwear.

Pantaloons were the preferred costume of a few early feminists. Amelia Jenks Bloomer, staunch member of the Women's Temperance Society, took on dress reform in 1853, wearing full-cut pantaloons under a knee-length skirt while she delivered her speeches. Her innovative attire was mocked and flopped as a fashion style, but Bloomer's name was forever linked with the pantaloon, probably not the legacy she preferred.

Pantaloons gave way to flesh-colored "trousers", which hugged the thighs a bit more and stopped at the knee, similar to the 19th-century bathing suit. Knee-stopping trousers climbed up higher when skirts rose after World War I. In the 1930s, women could finally slip into short, soft, silky underwear, like "camishorts" that buttoned down the side. Shorts shrank to briefs. Lightweight crepe de chine with ribbons and lace and silk or sateen turned underwear into lingerie.

KEEPING UP STANDARDS

"No person shall appear in a public street in said village unless his or her buttocks and the private and intimate parts of his or her body are covered with fully opaque covering. Violators are fined or imprisoned."
—DRESS CODE, SOUTHAMPTON, NEW YORK.

My Cup Runneth Over

Soft bras are the last great lingerie invention, perhaps because it's widely agreed that, given a boost from below, female breasts are perfect as they are. Who wants hard boobs? Certain late Victorians apparently did. Such women wore "bust improvers," twin-cupped wire structures that look like food strainers.

It wasn't until the 20th century that the true brassiere was born, both soft and supportive and usually comfortable, except for strapless designs that were trying to do the work of a corset, too. Other multi-task bras have included the "Mon-e-Bra," which was designed with a zippered section between the cups to hide big bucks or bijoux.

Not until Dior's "New Look" in 1947 declared curves back in, did most bra makers add much emphasis. Enter the pointy bras, the missiles and cones, worn by '40s and '50s sweater girls. Maidenform's legendary two-decade campaign, "I dreamed I was (a queen, a dancer, a toreador etc.) in my Maidenform bra" ended in 1969 but created a booming business for many bra makers—from luxe and pricey La Perla push-ups to Victoria Secret's gel-filled bras that "give you what nature didn't."

American women were encouraged to assume a patriotic, pointedly uplifting attitude in the 1940s.

INSIDE OUT

A couple of lifetimes ago, the white tee shirt was just army regulation underwear. Then, worn without an overshirt, it became a sexy bad-boy symbol, as long as a pack of Luckies was stuck in one rolled-up sleeve. Now the plain tee is a staple of any fashionable woman's closet.

Four decades ago, Helen Gurley Brown told readers of *Sex and the Single Girl* that nothing was sexier than letting a bit of lacy bra top "accidentally" peek out from a partially buttoned shirt. But Madonna wins the prize for really putting underwear out there. In the '80s, it was a cult thing: Madonna's gutsy

A Couture Moment: Jean-Paul Gaultier's corset dress in orange velvet

PHOTO BY IRVING SOLERO, COURTESY OF THE MUSEUM AT F.I.T., NEW YORK public undress style was known only to "in" New York club goers and people who'd seen the arty film, *Desperately Seeking Susan*. But Madonna won fans worldwide to her inside-out look when she appeared on stage in 1990 wearing little but her missile cone-shaped bra and corselette, with dangling garters, by Jean Paul Gaultier.

As for the bottom line, the g-string, once worn only by strippers, is now so yesterday for White House interns. Still, there are clingy dresses and pants, which, when viewed from behind, just can't afford the outline of undies. Only the crack-irritating thong bikini will work. So why bother with underpants at all? Some cite feminine delicacy. Others admit that anything worn underneath is sexy in a way that innerwear parading as outerwear can never be.

Final Take

"Hole onter sumpin' an' suck in yo' breaf."–Mammy (HATTIE MCDANIEL) to Scarlett O'Hara (VIVIEN LEIGH), *Gone with the Wind* (MGM),1939

CHAPTER SIX

Layers on

Dangereuse

Mark Twain wrote an article for *The Fashion Item* after he had attended an elegant reception in 1867, noting that "the most fashionably dressed lady was Mrs. G.C. She wore a pink satin dress, plain in front but with a good deal of rake to it—to the train, I mean; it was said to be two or three yards long. One could see it creeping along the floor some little time after the woman was gone."

At the turn of the 20th century, a woman's gown still looked like her living room curtains. Decorated with poufs of silk and satin, it covered an abundance of underskirts and, in the back, a bustle. Long trains like tails attached to the dresses invaded floor space and sidewalks. A fashionable woman would walk through the streets of the great cities, her gown trailing behind her, without noticing that her dress had become a broom.

In 1900, a physician named Casagrandi delivered a paper to the medical association in Rome. He revealed the results of his bacterial experiments on the debris attached to hemlines and discovered bits of chewed tobacco, a scrap of pork pie, cigar and cigarette ends, cat's meat, mud and some toothpicks. The collected germs represented large colonies of deadly tuberculosis, typhoid fever, influenza and tetanus. A veritable petrie dish of contagion.

Women couldn't easily run to the nearest dry cleaner after a day in town (there were only a few in cities), or even turn on the tub. Few homes had running water. Instead, fine clothing was relegated to

The Mysterious West: For centuries, fashionable European women were walking brooms. In this early 1600s painting, Zurbarán depicts a saint in the prevailing style.

SANTA CASILDA BY FRANCISCO DE ZURBARÁN, PRADO, MADRID

fresh air and careful brushing, but microscopic germs from rat fleas and lice, carriers of the plague and typhus, clung to hemlines.

It's a Wrap

What was good enough for the gods—who were said to have been clothed in the finest linen—was good enough for the Egyptians. Four thousand years ago, Egyptians worked the fabric into elegant ankle-length sheaths. The Greeks and, eventually, the Romans copied the styling for their togas and robes, made out of a single piece of fabric, draped into pleats and folds, and held in place by decorative pins.

Asians took the draped look one step further; their early improvisations included wrapping fabric around the hips and between the legs to form loose-fitting trousers.

Innovation on the subcontinent created the sari. One Indian legend tells of a beautiful wife lost in a gambling duel to a lecherous enemy. When the evil victor tried to unravel her diaphanous sari, there was no end to the fabric—a blessing bestowed on her by Lord Krishna.

Even the contemporary sari uses at least six yards of silk; it takes three weavers two weeks to a month to fabricate a handmade silk sari cloth, and much longer to weave the silk

Fashion's Dictates

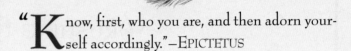

"Know, first, who you are, and then adorn yourself accordingly."—EPICTETUS

"If you are not in fashion, you are nobody."—LORD CHESTERFIELD

with intricate designs. The gossamer fabric folds closely around the woman. Traditional Indian women elegantly pleat and fold their saris without assistance from zippers, buttons or other fastening gizmos.

CRUSHING BEAUTY

There are no safety clasps on a kimono either, although its constricting bulk can move the wearer into a danger zone. Once bound up in the glorious garment, a woman is like a beautiful gift until unwrapped.

The traditional Japanese robe dates back to the Heian era (A.D. 794-1185), when ladies and gentlemen of the Japanese court wore twelve different layers of elaborate silk brocades, none of them the same pattern or color. This extraordinary dressing feat could only be accomplished with the talent of servants. Even an expert needs a half hour just to tie the 13-foot long *obi* (sash) that wraps round the reams of costly, beautiful brocades.

A simplified kimono is worn today on special occasions. On January 15, women of twenty have a "coming out" party in kimonos, sometimes worn with fur boas. Traditional tea parties, school graduations and some New Year's Eve festivities call for kimonos, and a kimono remains a wedding tradition. The bride begins the occasion in an embroidered red kimono, appears next in a white one, with an elaborate headpiece and oversized wig, for the exchange of vows, and finally dons a Western-style ball gown. Exhausting! Her groom gets away without changing his clothes. For the ceremony, he appears in a simple black silk kimono, which bears his family crest in white. Funerals are less demanding: both men and women wear plain black kimonos.

The modern Japanese woman usually rents her kimono, an expensive woven artwork, but ownership still confers the mystery and honor of ancient times.

The worth of a classically-trained geisha was reflected by the number and quality of kimonos she possessed. Her real power was called *keisie*—"castle toppler." It was said that a beautifully turned out geisha could overthrow a castle with a single flutter of her eyelashes.

A kimono artfully slows down the person in it—it's certainly not made for sprinting. The *obi*-bound layers restrict leg movement and flatten the chest, while an unarranged kimono is longer than the wearer is tall. The high platform shoes that accessorize the kimono are hazardous in themselves—but that's another chapter.

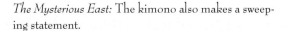

The Mysterious East: The kimono also makes a sweeping statement.

MEN IN GOWNS

BLUE RIBBON BRAGGART #6

It's surprising that some men in the late Middle Ages and Renaissance didn't pitch over from the sheer weight of their clothes. Men in some professions announced their prominence by dressing in long garments, some three times their body length. You could really make an entrance if you were a judge or a priest flaunting your position in your voluminous robe with train and heavy mantle.

In his first promenade as British prime minister, he wore an outfit typical of his wardrobe—light blue trousers, black stockings with red stripes, rings on his gloves—and remarked on the reaction of the people in the street: "It was like the parting of the Red Sea." —BENJAMIN DISRAELI (1804-1881)

The common serf wore simple clothing—spare and rough-woven tunics and leggings—the better to work in. But most professionals, including academics, liked to occupy lots of space in billowy gowns. One of the brainier men of the era, Galileo, was an exception. This professor of math refused to wear his academic robes, reported Dava Sobel in her biography of his daughter. He considered the prescribed clothing "a pretentious nuisance . . . the dignity of the professor's gown barred him from the brothel, denying him the evil pleasures of whoring . . . the gown even impeded walking, to say nothing of working."

Many professionals, as well as kings and clerics, wore robes. This man in black is a 17th-century lawyer.

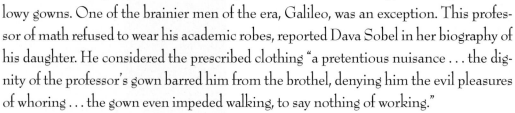

RUFFING IT

Even an impediment to eating can be a popular high-fashion item. Snooty nobles and some of their followers in the 16th and 17th centuries wore a "ruff" or collar that gave the optical illusion that the head was farther away from the body than in reality. The lace face-frame began as a modest trimming on a high-necked chemise. Its royal send-off as an ostentatious accessory was abetted by starch so it might stand up on its own.

Elizabethans favored the wide wrist ruff as well as the high lace collar, establishing a second barrier to neat dining.

Many narrow lace strips had to be sewn together and starched to make the stiff nine-inch collar required by fashion. Elizabeth I tackled the eating dilemma by splitting her ruff in the front, allowing her regal fingers to reach beyond it to get to her mouth. As the decades of her reign wore on, her exaggerated ruff rose to greater heights behind her head, framing her exquisite facial bones.

A man's ruff interfered with his long, curly hairstyles and made his head look as if it were being served on a plate. Short hair came into fashion, not to be lengthened again until the lace ruff collapsed into the soft, wide collars of *Three Musketeers* fame. These collars in turn gave way to other strangling neckpieces and became the lace jabot, the cravat and eventually the necktie.

Ruff Going: It wasn't easy to eat in a ruffled collar until Elizabeth I diminished the dilemma by slitting hers in half, as shown by the illustration top right.

Puff, Up and Away

Ribbons and feathers had long protruded from a gentleman's wardrobe when grotesquely puffed sleeves debuted in the 1500s. Henry VIII's taste in dress was as outsized as his penchant for disposable wives. The enormous puffed sleeve was called "puff and slash"—not a dueling term, but a contrast of one loud color peeking through a slash in the sleeve of a different color.

Henry VIII's puffed sleeve matched his short, velvet puffy pants and the pom-poms on his shoes. The wide lapel favored by the king and his copiers, along with their sashes and ribbons, made the richly decorated males look like clowns. The outfit was topped off with a beret the size of a pizza, with an ostrich plume sticking out of it. The extras were not pepperoni but embroidery and precious jewels.

A man's clothing added at least twenty pounds to his naked weight, which was not inconsiderable in the case of Henry VIII. It's hard to imagine a noble disguised as an overstuffed chair being nimble with either a sword or axe but, as we know, Hank left it to professionals to cut off his wives' heads.

When enormous puffed sleeves made their comeback in the early 1800s, in women's clothing, they were exaggerated still

Fancy Pants: The over-accessorized Elizabethan swain might choose black and white for his Spanish breeches. Almost a century later, French courtiers wore "petticoat breeches," trimmed with as much as 250 years of ribbon.

> *You beautiful ladies, that follow the mode,*
> *Where ever you live, or take up your abode,*
> *Pray what is the reason you wear such a load*
> *As hoop'd petticoats, monstrous petticoats,*
> *bouncing hoop'd petticoats?*
> —ANONYMOUS, 18th century

further. Cartoonists could not resist illustrating them as parachutes; it wasn't much of a reach.

These hugely inflated puffy sleeves were either designed with their padding as part of the dress or were supported by separate contraptions attached to the upper arms before the dress was draped over them. Little stuffed pillows or tiered lantern shapes were tied to the corset's shoulder straps. The impressive sleeves gave the illusion of a diminished waistline and a long neck.

Hot Air Apparel: The Victorians called these super-puffs for women and men leg-of-mutton sleeves.

Killer Skirts

DRAWING BY E. PREVAL AND P. DEHERNEVILLE, *ENGLISHWOMAN'S DOMESTIC MAGAZINE*, 1866

A hoop-skirted lady, standing still in a ballroom, took up as much as eight yards of floor space. She couldn't have swished around very much.

Hoops had other drawbacks. Almost any exertion could throw a woman of elegance off balance, with consequences ranging from the exposure, heaven forbid, of a petticoat or ankle, to falling out of a carriage. A strong wind could turn a hoop inside out while a woman was walking and knock a passerby squarely in the jaw.

Massive skirts, however they were held up, presented a clear and present danger both to the wearer and those who stood near her. The 19th-century French writer, Prosper Merimee, claimed to know 17 women who had stood too close to a fire to peer into a mirror over the mantle, only to have their billowing dresses catch fire. There are countless accounts of women studying a painting over the fireplace or just warming a cold shoulder and accidentally incinerating themselves. The highest body count attributed to expansive dress comes from Santiago, Chile, where, on December 8, 1863, a fired raged through the cathedral, killing 2,500 souls. The fire

Fashion Hazard: Women in hoop skirts were dangerous.

allegedly started after a woman lit a candle, which sparked onto her full-skirted dress, quickly passing to legions of other petticoats and the men who loved them.

Even before that fire, one crinoline manufacturer defensively advertised that his wares "do not cause accidents and do not appear at inquests."

Hoop skirts were blamed for an 1860s crime wavelet in Paris. The most unlikely goods—stolen umbrellas and, in another case, a cage with 40 pheasant chicks, were found under the perps' dresses.

On at least one occasion, however, big skirts saved lives. In May 1862, the *Hampshire Gazette* reported that ladies who fell out of a rowboat were kept afloat by their buoyant hoop skirts.

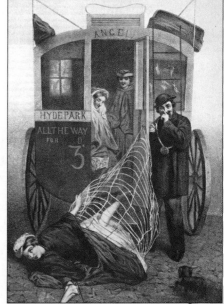

ACCESSORY ACCIDENTS

Although successive tidal waves of fabric apparently threatened those in vogue, for generation after generation, 20th- and 21st-century chic has not been without hazard. More often than not, the enemy has been a must-have accessory.

Flappers happily kicked up their exposed legs. But the length that had departed from the skirt came back as long strings of beads, feather boas and silk scarves to die for. While Isadora Duncan was riding in a top-down car in Nice on September 14,

1927, her smashingly long scarf danced in the wind behind her. Unfortunately, it caught in the vehicle's rear wheel and strangled Isadora to death.

People tend to notice potential self-abuse through their accessories—when attempting to clasp a tight, beaded choker or fasten a sharp collar pin, for example. But it's easy to overlook the dangers chic accessories pose to others. Caution signs should be posted in busses and trains until the enthusiasm for backpacks and over-the-shoulder satchel purses subsides. People deploying ten-plus-pound loads in any number of stylish ways could crush you between their weighty accessory and a bus pole, and they wouldn't even feel it.

And your punky friend in her biker jewelry—the bracelet with spikes or the heavy metal motor links—can slash you wide open with a flick of the wrist.

Picture Perfect

It's only human to want to dress up in an overabundance of finery, and it's natural to want that fine look recorded for others to admire. As Oscar Wilde put it, "You should either be a work of art or wear a work of art." Being in a work of art is an alternative, especially if you can demand that your portrait be painted, making you look taller, richer, and more beautiful or handsome than you are in real life. The ultimate vanity, after all, is immortality.

In Wilde's Faustian novel, *The Picture of Dorian Gray*, a handsome young Victorian is awed by the portrait painted of him: "The sense of his beauty came to him like a revelation." Then Dorian is struck by what his future might look like: "The scarlet would pass away from his

Egoist Checklist

FAVORITE FOOD	*Fish for compliments*
COMMON ILLNESS	*Swelled head*
CLOTHING SIZE	*Too big for his breeches*
POLITICAL POSITION	*Self-centered*
RELIGION	*Self-worship*
PREFERRED PETS	*Cock and crow*
FAVORITE RIDING HABIT	*Mounting his high horse*
FAVORITE EXERCISE	*Patting himself on the back*
FAVORITE AUTO PART	*Vanity plate*
CLIMATE PREFERENCE	*Hot air*
FAVORITE EXCURSION	*Ego trip*
FAVORITE PERFUMES	*"First" by Van Cleef & Arpel, "Remember Me" by Christian Dior*
FAVORITE MUSICAL PERFORMANCE	*Tooting his own horn*
MOST DIFFICULT SECRET TO KEEP	*Opinion of himself*
FAVORITE BOOK	*This one*

lips, and the gold steal from his hair . . . 'How sad it is! I shall grow old, and horrible and dreadful. But this picture will remain always young'."

In real life, the money to commission a portrait may come only with age. "Above all, show me as I am, claims each woman" who sits for a portrait, wrote a critic quoted in Aileen Ribeiro's *Ingres in Fashion*. "This really means, if it's an old woman, 'take twenty years off my age;' for the faded blonde, 'I insist on a fresh complexion;' the redhead says, 'make my hair a beautiful blonde;' the woman with a yellow skin wants it white; the hunchbacked woman cries, 'don't forget to hide my hump.'"

The historical record shows that men are no less vain, and some have both gun and purse power to enforce their whims—Josef Stalin, for example. The tyrant, whose ego

ꟻINAL ꟲAKE

"If I'm going to die, let me die well-dressed!"
—French Major Jean Villeneuve (TCHEKY KARYO), *The Patriot* (Columbia Pictures), 2000

was larger than his stature of only five-foot-four, wanted to be painted as a tall man "with hands that could uproot trees," in the words of historian Daniel McNeil. If the portraitist didn't comply, the artist was shot and the artwork burned.

CHAPTER SEVEN

TORTURED

SOLES

With a magic click of her ruby red heels, Dorothy was transported to safety. Cinderella's lost glass slipper did more for her than her billowy ball gown. And messages could be delivered at the speed of the wind if you contracted with Mercury, wings on his sandaled feet. But these foot fairy tales are no match for history.

Vanity and necessity are married in the world of shoes. Shoes not only keep your feet off rugged surfaces of gravel, cement, sand, rocks, hot asphalt and sheets of ice and snow; they also tell the world the kind of person you are: a practical soul or a fun-loving fashion victim.

In the landscape of the past, shoes announced status or profession. Monarchs and their courts wore lovely, embroidered slippers or colored leather shoes fastened with real jewels; slaves and servants went barefoot; and hunters and soldiers tramped in boots.

Above all, shoes have the seemingly magic ability to heighten us into imposing or seductive postures. But not without a price. Still, wearing the latest style high heels, is worth the Dr. Scholl's aftermath, the chiropractor, the aromatherapy pedicure, the anti-inflammatories and all the Band Aids in the medicine cabinet. The true sign of the brave woman is dancing all night in her backbreaking, toe-pinching stilettos. Fashion before comfort. But today's brave man wears Nikes with his tux—foregoing the etiquette of patent leather pumps.

The Winged Foot, as enjoyed by Mercury

First Steps

Ancient Egyptian sandals were made of woven or braided papyrus leaves—useful for walking in the desert sand but not that great in battle. To conquer the world, the Romans perfected a military sandal, studded on the bottom with nails, designed for long troop movements. One duty of a slave, who was generally not allowed to wear shoes at all, was to carry and untie the sandals of his master. In Mark (1:7), "John also told the people, "Someone more powerful is going to come. And I am not good enough even to stoop down and untie his sandals."

King Solomon in Song of Solomon (7:1) praised beautiful feet. He recognized pampered peds when he saw them: "How graceful are your feet in sandals, O queenly maiden," he tells Abishag, from the town of Shunem.

Flirty young women decorated their sandals with bells, although their elders disapproved. The Book of Isaiah (3:16) records their complaints: "Haughty daughters of Zion walking and mincing as they go and making a tinkling with their feet. The Lord will take away the bravery of their tinkling ornaments about their feet."

Siren Song

Glamorous Brazilian singer Carmen Miranda dragged suitcases full of cork wedgies to Hollywood. In 1955, the five-foot Miranda wore eight-inch wedgies when she belted out her hit song, *I Want To Be Tall*.

MORE OPEN AIR LOOKS

The foot has always been a candidate for both martyrdom and stardom. In 1525 B.C., the Egyptian queen Hatshepsut was a trendsetter who removed her elaborately jeweled sandals to bathe her feet in scented oils. Her well-tended feet boosted the sandal trade.

Egyptians liked to be buried with their sandals. Queen Ankhesenamum kept a pair of bark sandals in her tomb, with pictures of the pharaoh's enemies etched on the inside soles. Just in case they appeared, she could step on them.

Roman lovers took the soles of shoes very seriously and it became a custom for a mistress to present her lover with a token sandal. One of the first foot fetishists was the Roman Emperor Lucius Vitellius, who kept a shoe of his mistress under his tunic so he could kiss it whenever he felt the urge. Some devoted lovers used the shoe like a sky writer. A man carved the name of his lover into the sole of his shoe and left an imprint in the sand for her to witness his undying devotion—until a blow of sand came along and erased her name.

WHATEVER IS AFOOT

The primitive sandal looks very much like a modern one—stiff sole plus straps or a toe thong. In Japan and China, rice straw was worked for sandals; in South America, the leaves of the sisal plant were twined; in India, wood was used. The Australian Aborigines used tree bark.

A glacier-preserved Stone Age man, discovered in the Alps in 1991, still had his shoes. If he was typical of his culture in 3300 B.C., the European style apparently was to fashion a shoe of untanned leather insulated with grass. Other primitive peoples, who lived in frigid climates, wrapped animal skins around the feet like bags. Traditional Russian boots were made of goat's wool woven into a cold-resistant felt, while Tibetans kept their feet warm with yak hair. Native Americans found the soft deerskin boot or moccasin best for sneaking up on their prey.

Lily Feet

BSM's 2001 EXHIBITION, BATA SHOE MUSEUM, TORONTO.

Nowhere were there more binding standards for what constitutes beauty in a feminine foot than among the upper classes in China. And the idea of pretty feet was intricately wrapped up with the implicit presumption of uselessness. A woman's feet should be delicate in the extreme to be attractive, and render her too helpless to run.

Foot binding, the story goes, began in the 10th century after a Chinese prince fell in love with the minute "lily feet" of his concubine; for the next 1,000 years the feet of aristocratic young girls were tightly bound; the results would symbolize their gentility and beauty. Starting at age three, tiny girls had their feet lovingly

For real, live dolls: Late 19th-century shoes for the Chinese woman whose feet had been bound.

washed in hot water before their toes were turned under and cruelly pressed against the bottoms of their feet. The arches were broken so the foot was in line with the leg, then the foot was bound with cotton to hold the position. The bandages were tightened every day until the foot was miniaturized. This extreme beautifying process restricted blood circulation; sometimes toes fell off.

Some perfectly shrunk adult female feet could fit into embroidered silk shoes only three or four inches long. These "lotus shoes" were tiny showcases of fine needlework, with birds and flowers embroidered on expensive silks and velvets, the heels carved from the wood of the pomegranate or lycee tree. There were 18 styles of "lotus shoes." The passages of a woman's life could be followed through her shoe collection: peony motifs for spring, mandarin ducks for marital happiness (because they mate for life), grapes sewn on apple green silk to enhance her chances of bearing many sons.

Men found the tiny steps of women with bound feet refined and erotic. Women with doll feet moved around best on their knees, bowing to the conformity of cultural pressure, as some women bow today to back-wrenching, high-fashion spikes.

The equation, admittedly, is imperfect: foot binding was compulsory and painful, with permanent consequences. Still, the Chinese girl, proud of her beautiful little feet, knew she had better marry well enough to be guaranteed a sedan chair, just as the modern stiletto-heeled maiden may live in hope of a chauffeured limousine. But once installed in the back seat, at least today she can kick off her shoes and wiggle her toes.

SOLE-FUL TALE

Bound feet, bound feet,
past the gate can't retreat.
—CHINESE DITTY

Reaching New Heights

Men, as well as women, have favored high heels to boost height. Ancient Greek thespians wore clogs to raise them above audiences. To keep their feet free of the dust of unpaved streets and the puddles of public baths, women of the Ottoman Empire chose elevated footwear called *kabkabs*. These 19th-century stilted sandals were made of fine boxwood or ebony, hardy woods durable in damp conditions. Those inlaid with mother-of-pearl or silver were packed away for trousseaus or kept for special occasions.

For centuries, the Japanese have been wearing various forms of high wooden platform shoes, whose designs indicated whether they were part of the Imperial household, merchants or actors. Emperor Hirohito wore high platform *getas* at his coronation in 1926.

During the Edo period (1603-1867), high-polish prostitutes would parade slowly in public wearing

East or West: Height gives glamour and authority.

extravagant kimonos and *takagetas*, clogs that could be a ridiculous 30 inches high. Such a geisha walked with the help of an attendant to keep her from falling over.

In 1430, the Venetian government prohibited pregnant women from wearing popular thick wooden stilts, called *chopines*, attached to their shoes—apparently because several high-born, high ladies had toppled, provoking miscarriages. In spite of the ban, 16th-century women of leisure continued to wear the high-style *chopine*. A lady in *chopines* needed two assistants to steady her. The style made short women tall, and tall women giants.

The high-platform shoe has reappeared in Europe and America, but not with quite the stature it once had. In Japan, however, the style is high-rise enough to cause modern accidents. One day in 2000, a 25 year-old Tokyo woman, Tommomi Okawa, was driving home from shopping when she crashed her car into a concrete pole, killing a friend sitting in the passenger seat. Ms. Okawa was wearing six-inch-high platform boots and couldn't brake properly, police said.

The Japanese citizen is no longer allowed to wear a kimono with sandal getas while operating a vehicle. That safety rule, of course, does not prevent pedestrian fatalities. Misayo Shimizu, who

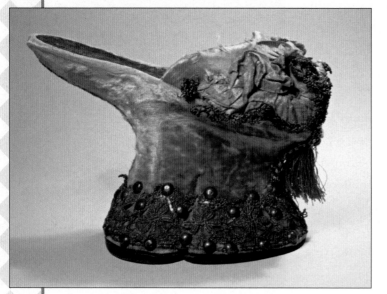

There Was a Law Against Them: A gold velvet chopine.

worked in a nursery school, tripped while wearing four-inch-high cork clogs, fell, fractured her skull and died. But this widely-reported stumble has not cooled the fashion rage in Tokyo. Many petite Japanese women like viewing the world from their platform perspective—apparently a trip to the orthopedist is worth looking a guy in the eye.

High heels and ill-fitting shoes are also blamed for most trips and falls in the United States. Exactly where? Off the curb.

Fashion models' occupational hazards include sashaying down slick runways. During Gucci's 2002 fall collection show, a British model, wearing four-inch heels, staggered and fell twice. Surrendering to comfort, she tossed aside her shoes and continued to model barefoot; she barely kept her career going.

> "If you want to forget your problems, wear tight shoes."
> —EUROPEAN PROVERB

ROYAL RED

In 2300 B.C. Syria, leather was dyed red for the first time by the Phoenicians and they liked the look. The color obtained from the juice of crushed beetles was a favorite.

Spartans wore red boots to hide the blood from their wounds.

Julius Caesar caused a stir in the Roman Senate when he appeared wearing red boots with

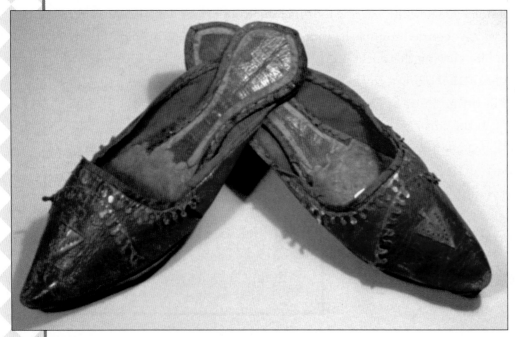

Royal Red: These 1,700-year-old leather shoes with gold leaf detailing still look classy.

COPTIC, BATA SHOE MUSEUM, TORONTO.

high heels. Red was reserved for the young at that time, but the aging Caesar insisted it was the fashion of his ancestors, the kings of Alba.

Nero stripped the red boots off senators who were suspected of being Christians. He took an even greater interest in the shoe stash of his wife, Poppaea, ordering Imperial shoemakers to fashion for her shoes with silver soles and a pair with gold soles, and straps encrusted with rare gems. Even Nero's horses galloped around in gold horseshoes. But Nero had a temper. Clad in his own sandals made of poured gold, he kicked poor Poppaea to death.

For a while, red was the designated color of Roman magistrates. But Emperor Marcus Aurelius declared only he and his successors could wear red sandals.

Both Ghengis Khan and Louis XVI preferred red heeled shoes for entertaining.

Off With Their Heels

Heels may increase a woman's field of vision but, in colonial America, men thought they were the devil's work. Following the import of Parisian high-heeled shoes for women in 1670, the colony of New Jersey passed this stiletto law:

All women, whether virgins, maidens, or widows, who shall after this Act impose upon, seduce or betray into matrimony any of his Majesty's male subjects by virtue of . . . high heel shoes shall incur the penalty of the law now in force against witchcraft, sorcery, and such . . . [and] the marriage shall stand null and void.

Men in Heels

High heels also elevate public image. Short Louis XIV pranced around in five-inch, red cork heels decorated with miniature battle scenes. Louis XV also flaunted his footwear. He owned shoes that cost a year's salary for a peasant. The "Louis" heel, still used today, was a sturdy one with a nipped in midsection. The elegant toe was moderately pointy. Most shoes were heavily embroidered with silk, satin and gold threads, and closed with jeweled buckles or extravagant ribbon bows.

Pretty Feet: These white kid shoes appliquéd with silver lace and silk ribbon helped a fellow cut a swell figure back in 1690.

If The Shoe Doesn't Fit, Wear It Anyway

All shoes were necessarily handmade for most of fashion history. For a proper fit, the client's feet had to be duplicated in size and form with a "footprint" from which a wooden mold, called a last, was made. A different last is required for each shoe style whether it's handmade or mass-produced.

A proper foot tracing results in left and right shoes. But, oddly, between 1830 and 1860, many shoes were made on absolutely straight lasts. There was no difference between the right and left soles. Moreover, narrow feet set the standard of beauty and sizing. Commercially manufactured shoes were, in fact, called "straights." Slipping one's feet into a dainty pair of fabric slippers wasn't so bad. But breaking in a new pair of leather shoes was not easy. The foot was supposed to adjust to the shoe and not the other way around. Some owners of store-bought shoes were cautioned to remember to rotate each shoe between left and right foot. Even so, wearing "straights" resulted in a grievous list of deformities like bunions, corns, hammertoes and ingrown nails.

Because shoes, made-to-order or not, were expensive, families handed down pairs from child to child. In some cases, good Sunday shoes were bequeathed to the next generation.

Shoe size and fit, of course, have limited roles in fashion, even today. Mass production just meant we had more styles to choose among. Eighty-eight per cent of women today buy shoes one size too small just because they like them.

Getting a Grip

The felt precursor of the sneaker crept into the world by royal command. Henry VIII decided he needed exercise so he summoned his valet to find him "syxe paire of shooys with feltys, to pleye in at tennys."

Centuries later, Charles Goodyear was fiddling with a rubber mixture in his kitchen to come up with one that would adhere to canvas mailbags. As he shook the mixture, a glob flew out and landed on the stove. The heat transformed it. Eureka—a vulcanized rubber had been created that wouldn't turn gummy in the summer or brittle in the winter. In 1868, Goodyear produced the first white canvas sneakers. They sold for $6.00 a pair, too much money for the average Joe, but worth it to the idle rich who needed play shoes, which they called croquet sandals.

When U.S. Rubber bought Charles Goodyear's business they reproduced the little white sneakers, renamed them Keds and, in 1897, sold them in catalogues for sixty cents a pair. The sales footrace greatly accelerated after 1972, when a track coach named Bill Bowerman shaped rubber in his waffle iron at home and invent-

Head of the Army by William Heath, 1827

A WELLINGTON BOOT
or the Head of the Army.

ed the traction waffle sole for the sneakers marketed by his new company, Nike.

Monikers for dozens of different kinds of sports shoes aside, no shoe has inspired more nicknames than the sneaker. They've been called felonies, perp boots, brothel creepers and gumshoes (in honor of the quiet and speed they lend to various activities), as wells as plimsolls. (Samuel Plimsoll sponsored legislation in 1876 that required ships to be marked with water-lines—like the blue lines that appeared on sneakers.)

Mulish Behaviors

The mule is the bikini of shoes. In the fashion world of the foot, there actually is something called "toe cleavage." The backless mule is hot because it exposes more foot flesh than most styles.

But other "naked" versions have their fans. Ever since a press shoot to publicize *The Seven Year Itch*, during which Marilyn Monroe's white dress blew up to her neck, concentrating attention on her exposed legs and barely there high-heeled sling-backs, strappy sandals have been sexy.

Andy Warhol thought there was nothing sexier than a woman working the room in a pair of killer-high stilettos and drop-dead red toenails. In his little book, *Shoes, Shoes, Shoes*, he asserted, "You can impress a whole room full of people and maybe with any luck you'll never see them again."

Collecting sexy footwear has a long history. Owning many shoes has nothing to do, of course, with *needing* them. Empress Josephine owned 521 pairs of slippers—and wore each pair

only once. Sara Vass, a serious shoe collector, who owns just as many pairs as Josephine, believes, "If your body lets you down, your feet will still lift your spirits."

But few shoe fanciers can compete with the first lady of sole, Imelda Marcos, whose expropriated collection of 1200 pairs is displayed in a Manila museum to give a kick to tourism. When Imelda and her disgraced husband fled the Philippines in 1986, she wore a comfy pair of blue canvas espadrilles. Among the stompers left behind in the palace closet were five pairs of identical black Charles Jourdans, with rhinestone-studded spike heels. Mrs. Marcos had brought an old shoe adage to a new level ("when you find a shoe you love, buy it every color"); she just bought the same color again and again.

The Fetish shoe store in Austin, Texas offers an Imelda discount: if you buy five pairs of shoes (they cost between $160-$340), you get one pair free.

Sole Searcher Timeline

3000 B.C. —Aphrodite, love goddess and first pinup girl, is pictured naked except for her sandals.

1343 B.C. —Tutankhamen is entombed with papyrus-soled gold sandals inlaid with colored glass and tied with straps, which depict a Nile scene of enameled-gold lotus and ducks.

500 B.C. —Harsiotef, king of Ethiopia, takes inscribed sandals with him to the world beyond. Hieroglyphics read: "Ye have trodden the impure peoples under your powerful foot."

1096 —Crusader Shoe Fight. What, you don't have my size? For the long trek to the Holy Land, shoes are precious. A fight breaks out in Hungary between shoe merchants and potential buyers that spreads into an argument leaving 4000 dead.

1300s —Long Feet Prevail. Fashion fop Richard II of England and his crowd adopt a long-toed shoe that sticks out as much as two feet. To help knights mosey along, each end is tied to a leg.

1745 —Madame de Pompadour, who has tiny feet, popularizes high, narrow "Pompadour" heels.

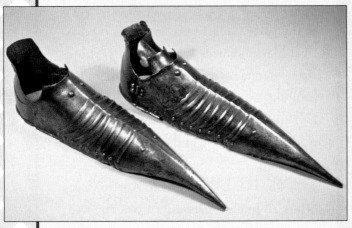

1490–What goes with my suit of armor? These steel sabatons solved a German nobleman's problem

Ladies with large feet tape down their toes to reduce their foot size and squeeze into small shoes like Mme. Pompadour's. But they faint in court.

1956 — Elvis Presley: "One for the money, two for the show . . ." *Blue Suede Shoes* tops the pop charts but fail to become a fashion trend.

1969 — Neil Armstrong rides Apollo II to the moon, stepping out in 25-layer (some of metal weave and Teflon) boots. When his four-inch thick asbestos soles touch the powdery moon surface he broadcasts back to earth: " One small step for man . . ."

1977 — Emperor Bokassa of the Central African Empire commissions an $85,000 pair of pearl-studded shoes from Berlutti for his coronation.

2003 — The average American woman owns 30 pairs of shoes, most of them uncomfortable.

Fancy Footwork

The fancy footwork of 20th-century Italian designer Salvatore Ferragamo landed on the feet of the royal and the rich, movie stars and dictators. World War I leather shortages forced Ferragamo to use alternatives, including cellophane, braided raffia and even paper with golden threads. "There is no limit to beauty, no saturation point in design, no end to the materials a shoemaker may use to decorate his creations so that every woman may be shod like a princess and a princess may be shod like a fairy queen," said Ferragamo.

THE
MOMENTUM
PROJECT

SPIKE HEAVEN AND HELL

There is little quite like a Manolo Blahnik spike. When Blahnik designed six pairs of gold shoes for Antonio Berardi's 1999 clothing collection, the shoes had their own bodyguards during the show. No wonder. They cost $9,944 a pair. Madonna, Faye Dunaway and Winona Ryder, among other stars, stand up (or wobble) in his gilded creations.

But Blahnik was outshone during the 2002 Oscar ceremonies when bodyguards came backstage to protect the world's first pair of diamond and platinum heels with a tag of $1 million. Actress Laura Harring (*Mulholland Drive*) slipped into the sparkling stilettos designed by Stuart Weitzman, who made this accessory versatile. The 464 single carats and two five-carat pear-shaped diamonds can be removed and

BLUE RIBBON BRAGGART # 7

1ST PLACE

"How tall am I? Honey, with hair, heels and attitude I'm through this damned roof."–RuPaul, female impersonator

worn as a necklace and a bracelet. How sensible.

High heels remain extremely popular because of the stature and glamour they impart to a woman. That sexy, powerful, look-at-me attitude is worth the risks to the back and legs. The pose that we strike in high heels forces the lower back to arch, the chest to protrude, and the fanny to stick out 25 per cent farther than if we were standing barefoot. Plus the look of our legs is lengthened. A woman in heels is basically falling forward, heaving herself out of her own shoes. But she may certainly catch the eye of a man who finds this unbalanced act fetching.

Too bad the body in the shoes doesn't like it. Standing at an angle for hours contracts a woman's Achilles' tendons and shortens the muscles in the backs of her legs, which can play havoc with her spine.

Like a marathon runner, high-heel devotees are encouraged to do hamstring stretches before and after wearing the spikes. Bend and stretch.

But even boots with modest heels can be a problem for cowboys. Contrary to popular belief, their frequent bow-leggedness comes not from riding their horses but from their boots. A man's hipbones are set differently than a woman's, causing his legs to bow when his boot heels force him to pitch forward.

FINAL TAKE

"And remember, never let those ruby slippers off your feet for a moment, or you'll be at the mercy of the Wicked Witch of the West." —Glinda (BILLIE BURKE) warning Dorothy (JUDY GARLAND), *The Wizard of Oz* (MGM), 1939

VOLUME I

VOLUME II

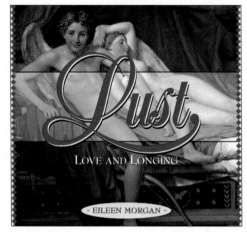

VOLUME III

Have you read...

VOLUME IV

VOLUME V